THE ROUG

GW00739156

Euro 2004

by
Dan Goldstein & Matthew Hancock

www.roughguides.com

ROUGH
GUIDES

Author: Dan Goldstein & Matthew Hancock
Editor: Peter Buckley
Layout: Dan Goldstein
Managing editor: Andrew Lockett
Production: Peter Buckley, Julia Bovis
Photography: Empics, Nottingham, England
With special thanks to the RSSSF Archive for statistical details,
and Paul Elbro and Andrew Barmford for Portuguese beer research.

....

This second edition published 2004 by **Rough Guides Ltd**, 80 Strand, WC2R 0RL
Distributed by the Penguin Group
Penguin Books Ltd, 80 Strand, London WC2R 0RL
Penguin Putnam Inc., 345 Hudson Street, NY 10014, USA
Penguin Books Australia Ltd, 487 Maroondah Highway, PO Box 257, Ringwood, Victoria 3134,
  Australia
Penguin Books Canada Ltd, 10 Alcorn Avenue, Toronto, Ontario, Canada M4V 1E4
Penguin Books (NZ) Ltd, 182–190 Wairau Road, Auckland 10, New Zealand

Printed in Italy by LegoPrint

A catalogue record for this book is available from the British Library
ISBN 1-84353-366-9

....

with special thanks to
Andrew Balmford
for fifteen years of
discovery together
x

Contents

Introduction

It may not have quite the global appeal or the glamour of the World Cup, but in many ways **the European Championship** is a more intriguing football tournament. There are fewer one-sided matches. The overall standard of the teams is higher. And the very fact that it does not come saddled with the months of build-up and hype which have come to blight the World Cup makes it somehow more approachable, more 'real'.

This year the final rounds of the Championship come to Portugal, a football destination that is about as 'real' as they come. The nation has played a key role in the evolution of the modern game, and its football history is littered with evocative, almost romantic names. Today's Portuguese players continue to uphold the tradition of a sophisticated, quick pass-and-move style, whether they are turning out for their country or for some of the richest club sides in Europe.

Yet for all the modernity of its football, Portugal has not succumbed to the crass over-commercialisation seen elsewhere in Europe. *Futebol* is a game almost everyone can afford to go and watch. Club members gather in traditional neighbourhood bars, not themed restaurants. Top-flight (*I Divisão*) teams happily wear lilac away strips; they may not be a marketable fashion accessory, but they are traditional.

As a travel destination, too, Portugal can seem to be stuck in something of a time warp, and is none the worse for it. The pace of life is relaxed. Eating out is cheaper than staying in. Crime rates are low. Above all, there is an eccentricity about the place that is hard to define but hugely enjoyable all the same. You know you are somewhere different.

Not that time is standing still in Portugal. A fully paid-up member of the European Union and a participant in the eurozone from the beginning, the country has emerged from decades of isolation and poverty. Today's Portuguese – younger generations, especially – have a stylish confidence about them.

This is reflected in the way the Portuguese have gone about the business of staging Euro 2004. Rather than try to refurbish grand old arenas such as Lisbon's Luz and José Alvalade, the organisers have commissioned all-new stadia notable for their spectacular use of colour, as well as for the way they subtly evoke the architectural legacy of the grounds they have replaced.

There is every sign that the football at Euro 2004 will live up to their unique style of its backdrop. As host nation, Portugal begin as one of the favourites, and the pedigree of the current side is beyond reproach. The holders, France, look to have put their calamitous World Cup of two years ago behind them. Italy, Spain, Holland and the Czech Republic all played some scintillating football en route to the finals. England, Germany, Russia and the Scandinavian teams will all be deftly organised and physically strong.

This Rough Guide to Euro 2004 does not pick a winner from among the 16 participating countries. Instead, we offer an insight into what makes each team tick – their history as a footballing nation, their road to the finals, their style, their strengths and their weaknesses. We also offer a detailed overview of the eight Portuguese towns and cities that will host the tournament. Finally, our Context section puts the whole thing into a cultural, historical and statistical perspective.

Whether you are looking forward to Euro 2004 as a travelling supporter or as an armchair fan, let the Rough Guide be your guide…

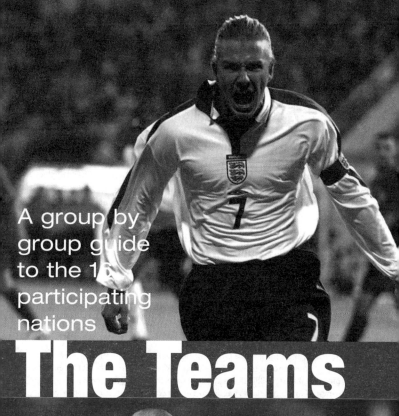

A group by
group guide
to the 16
participating
nations

The Teams

Group A: Greece

The Greeks enter these European Championship finals much as they did in 1980 – unheralded, unfancied and largely unloved. While the underdog-fanciers continue to fête little Latvia, the glamour vultures circle France, Italy, Spain and Portugal, and the likes of Russia and the Czech Republic fulfil their customary 'dark horse' roles, Greece appear to be doing little more than making up the numbers.

Part of the problem is the squad's apparent lack of star quality. Few if any of the Greek players are household names beyond their nation's borders, despite the fact that many earn their living in the continent's high-profile leagues. Not even the appointment of a big-name foreign coach, Otto Rehhagel, has aroused much public or media interest elsewhere in Europe.

Yet while it may be tempting to view the Greeks as also-rans, nobody should be in any doubt that the current side is determined to make an impact at Euro 2004 – or that it lacks the skill and organisation necessary to prove the sceptics wrong. The team qualified impressively from an awkward group, and the mere fact that they are being under-estimated will almost certainly work in their favour when they kick-off the tournament against hosts Portugal on 12 June.

Who they are

Another fly in the ointment of Greece's PR machine is the country's lack of pedigree at international level. When the Greeks qualified for the **European Championship finals of 1980**, it was the first time they had ever graced a major tournament. Coach Alketas Panagoulias encouraged his team to play fast and furious, and Greece – considered rank outsiders at the start of the competition – quickly won the hearts of their Italian hosts, coming close to an upset against the Netherlands in their first match, and holding eventual winners West Germany to a goalless draw in their last.

Fourteen years later, Panagoulias took a more experienced side to the USA for Greece's first and so far only World Cup finals. The veteran coach, who had returned to his homeland from a spell working in the States, urged his charges to draw inspiration from the **heroes of Greek mythology**, but the team's ageing stars were no match for younger opposition from Nigeria, Argentina and Bulgaria. Greece lost all three of their matches and failed to score a single goal.

Since then, the national side has consistently under-performed – despite a huge increase in the number of Greek stars playing top-class football abroad, and the maturing of the country's top club sides – Olympiakos, Panathinaikos and AEK Athens – into credible contenders at UEFA Cup and Champions League level.

How they got here

Even in Greece itself, few fans held out much hope for Euro 2004 qualification after the national team had begun its Group 6 campaign with a 2–0 home loss to Spain and a defeat by the same score in the Ukraine. It wasn't just the results that were poor; the Greeks were **outplayed in both games** and, at that stage, even a play-off berth looked beyond Rehhagel's side.

Four days after their defeat in Kiev, however, Greece enjoyed a comfortable 2–0 home win over Armenia, and when a nine-man Northern Ireland were beaten by the same score in Belfast in April 2003, confidence began to return.

The campaign's critical moment came with the return fixture against Spain in Zaragoza. Rehhagel **switched to a sweeper system** in the hope that a spare

Goalkeeper Antonios Nikopolidis marshalls one of Europe's meanest defences

man at the back would shackle the home side's Raúl and, while the Spaniards enjoyed the bulk of possession, their attack was made to look toothless for much of the game. Just before half-time and against the run of play, Stylianos Giannakopoulos scored a spectacular goal that proved enough to bag the Greeks all three points.

It was a similar story at home to Ukraine four days later, when a late goal by substitute Angelos Charisteas took Greece to the **top of the group table**, Spain having been held to a goalless draw by Northern Ireland the same day.

Further **1–0 victories** away to Armenia and at home to Northern Ireland – the former thanks to a Zizis Vryzas header, the latter courtesy of a Vassilios Tsartas penalty – sealed Greece's first place in the qualifying section and their place in the finals of Euro 2004.

How they'll play

With a relatively small group of international players and coach Rehhagel apparently anxious to keep a settled side, the Greek team will come closer than many at Euro 2004 to selecting itself. Antonios Nikopolidis is **Mr Reliable** between the sticks, although like so many consistent goalkeepers, he leaves something of a vacuum behind him in terms of a credible second choice.

The run of clean sheets that took Greece to the finals owed much to Nikopolidis' instinctive shot-stopping, but it also owed a good deal to the **solidity of the defence** in front of him, where Traianos Dellas, Giourkas Seitaridis, Stylianos Venetidis and Nikos Dabizas will be among the names to watch.

In midfield, Rehhagel puts the emphasis on **pressing the opposition** rather than keeping the ball for long periods. Skipper Theodoros Zagorakis and Angelos Basinas are the key men here, running their socks off from holding positions while the likes of Giannakopoulos, Vryzas and Vassilios Lakis enjoy greater freedom, often taking up wide positions in anticipation of a counter-attacking opportunity. With contemporary Greek game plans putting the emphasis on 'a good engine', younger players such as Akis Zikos and Ieroklis Stoltidis may also have a part to play.

On paper, Charisteas and Themis Nikolaidis look a promising strike partnership, but in reality both men often seem happier performing **a lone forward's role** – a part that Giannakopoulos and Vryzas can also play if called upon.

Who calls the shots

It was England who were the first opponents to get a real taste of what Otto Rehhagel might achieve as coach of the Greek national side. Needing only a point from their last qualifier at Old Trafford to be sure of a place at the 2002 World Cup finals, Sven Göran Eriksson's team trailed twice to **Rehhagel's lively, well-organised Greece** before David Beckham stepped up to curl in his immortal, last-gasp free-kick equaliser.

That was back in October 2001. Two-and-a-half years later, and the Hellenic football federation's decision to appoint Rehhagel looks inspired. Though he had never coached outside his native Germany before, 'King Otto' had a long track record of getting relatively **weak teams to play above themselves**. In both the *Bundesliga* and in European club competition, he worked wonders on a budget with the likes of Fortuna Düsseldorf, Werder Bremen and Kaiserslautern.

Werder won the European Cup-Winners' Cup in 1992, while Kaiserslautern won the German second-division title and the *Bundesliga* championship in successive years in 1997 and '98. By contrast, a brief spell trying to bang heads together in the millionaires' dressing room at Bayern Munich ended with the sack – even though what was essentially Rehhagel's team subsequently went on to win the UEFA Cup.

As **quick to innovate tacitcally** as he is to keep faith with the players who deliver for him, Rehhagel has moulded Greece into a team that encapsulates all the qualities he values: flexibility, resilience, solidity, and fear of absolutely nobody.

Portugal

Anyone wondering what to expect from Portugal during Euro 2004 needs only to have watched Cristiano Ronaldo a few times. On their day, both the national team and Manchester United's teenage progidy can ruthlessly torment the opposition with a dazzling array of skills. Equally, both can be physically lightweight, with a tendency to over-elaborate and fall flat on their face in front of goal.

The question of which Portugal shows its face during this summer's competition will be heavily influenced by the experience of coach Luiz Felipe Scolari, who saw it all while in charge of the winning Brazilian national side at the last World Cup. As with Brazil, Scolari is burdened by the expectation that his team is one of the tournament favourites, while also being faced with the task of blending together a bunch of superstars with some promising youngsters.

The biggest hope for Portugal is home advantage. With a good start, the crowd will be right behind the team and confidence is bound to surge, especially if home-based players such as Benfica striker Simão and Porto playmaker Deco turn it on. Then again, anything but a perfect start in the opening fixture against Greece, particularly if it is followed by a below-par display against Russia, may result in the home fans turning against their heroes, and the Portuguese suffering a calamity even greater than their premature exit from the 2002 World Cup...

Who they are

Portugal did not emerge as a force in international football until the country's biggest club side, Benfica, began to challenge Real Madrid's monopoly of the European Cup in the early 1960s. Benfica's star player was the striker Eusébio who, like many of the country's top players at the time, hailed from **one of Portugal's former colonies** (in his case Mozambique) rather than the country itself.

After leading Benfica to Europe's top club honour in 1961 and '62, Eusébio seized his moment on the global stage at the 1966 World Cup, inspiring Portugal to third place in what was the nation's first appearance in the finals. The team's victories included a symbolic 3–1 win over holders Brazil (itself a former Portuguese colony) and it took a couple of classic Bobby Charlton strikes at Wembley to halt Portugal's progress at the semi-final stage.

During the 1970s, Portugal's colonies gradually achieved independence, halting the flow of new talent into the national team and ensuring that the country did not reappear at a major finals until the European Championship of 1984. There, a brilliantly inventive side driven by the **impetuous goal-poaching** of Paulo Futre played

Has the lack of competitive opposition undermined Portugal's build-up to the tournament they're set to host?

out a classic semi-final with hosts France in Marseilles, losing 3–2 after extra time. At the Mexico World Cup two years later, a **row over bonus payments** between players and management crushed Portuguese hopes after the team had beaten England in their opening game.

Fresh hope sprang in the form of victories in the World Youth Cup in 1989 and '91 – the latter in front of 120,000 adoring fans at Lisbon's Stadium of Light. It was these Under-20 sides that would provide the basis for today's 'Golden Generation' of players such as Luís Figo, Manuel Rui Costa, Fernando Couto and João Pinto. Their first appearance in a major finals, in England at Euro '96, was ended by Karel Poborsky's wonder-chip for the Czech Republic in the quarter-finals. Four years later, a brilliant comeback win over England inspired a run to the semi-finals, where Abel Xavier's **infamous handball on the goal line** gifted France victory with a penalty in sudden-death extra time.

At the 2002 World Cup, a 4–0 romp over Poland was book-ended by seemingly inexplicable defeats at the hands of the USA and co-hosts South Korea. Portugal coach António Oliveira resigned, but **the blame for Portugal's early exit** surely lay at the feet of the European club season which, having raised the profile of Portuguese players to unprecedented heights, had robbed the Golden Generation of the energy it needed to show the world how talented it really was.

How they got here

Portugal have qualified for the finals automatically as hosts, but the decision to award the finals to the country was **not without controversy** when it was taken in 1998. Spain had put in a counter-bid with obvious commercial attractions, given the amount of money floating around in *La Liga*, the number of world-class arenas already built and the ease of travel to and around the country. Meanwhile, Austria and Hungary mounted a joint bid which appealed to UEFA's sense of political timing – the symbolism of uniting a member of the EU with a former Eastern Bloc country was hard to ignore.

In the end, though, the Portuguese delegation – expertly led by Eusébio himself – persuaded UEFA that the finals should be used as the means to rebuild a great European footballing power that had fallen on hard times. Portugal's great arenas such as the Stadium of Light were **crumbling with neglect**. Many fans, fed up with the predictability of the domestic game and disillusioned by a string of corruption scandals which tainted it during the 1990s, openly switched their allegiance to clubs in Spain or elsewhere. By awarding Euro 2004 to Portugal, Eusébio argued, UEFA would give the country a unique chance to put its house back in order.

On paper the strategy seems to have worked. With the help of substantial government funding, the Portuguese have built eight stunning new stadia, including all-new replacements for the Stadium of Light and the homes of the country's two other grand old clubs, Sporting Lisbon and FC Porto. Just as importantly, a string of infrastructure improvements, including major road projects and high-speed rail links between host cities, will make Portugal an easier place to travel around than it has ever been.

The question now is whether the Golden Generation, in what is probably its last great opportunity to win a major honour, can live up both to the colour, modernity and **romance of the tournament's setting**, and to its own star billing. As is customary for host nations, Portugal have been desperately trying to arrange meaningful friendlies against top-level opposition but have met with only limited success. Meanwhile, the demands of the European club season have scarcely diminished since the World Cup disaster two years ago, and there must be some doubt as to whether Euro 2004 will see Scolari's side perform at their best.

How they'll play

Most of the Golden Generation are now well into their thirties. Figo has already hinted this will be his last international tournament, while there is talk that Rui Costa will shortly leave Italy to see out his days at the club where he started, Benfica, suggesting his best days are behind him. But for Euro 2004, these golden oldies are being joined by a crop of **experienced younger players** and some fresh-faced upstarts that could, if the blend is right, make the tournament a swansong for the older generation.

The likes of Capucho, Pauleta and Jorge Andrade all appeared in the last World Cup and, like the bulk of the Golden Generation, these players will bring with them the experience of playing with successful European clubs. What remains to be seen is how Portugal's brightest youngsters will fit into the equation. Cristiano Ronaldo and Ricardo Queresma have done enough at Manchester United and Barcelona respectively to warrant a part in the competition, while Porto's promising right-back Paulo Ferreiro has had rave reviews. But other talents such as Hélder Postiga and Hugo Viana have been unable to make an impact away from Portugal.

A packed midfield and **aggressive defensive stance** have been the trademark of Scolari's teams in the past, and though this approach is unlikely to go down well with Portuguese supporters used to out-and-out attacking football, it could be a successful strategy. The likes of Andrade and Couto aren't afraid to rough up the opposition, and if Luis Boa-Morte gets a game, the team will have plenty of physical presence to complement the finer skills of Figo and Rui Costa.

Who calls the shots

Luiz Felipe Scolari has spent most of his two-decade long coaching career in his native Brazil. A journeyman professional player, he coached Grêmio to Copa Libertadores glory in 1995, and repeated the feat with Palmeiras four years later.

When Scolari was handed the reins of the Brazilian national side in 2001, he was the fourth coach to take charge of the team during the qualifying campaign for the 2002 World Cup. One English pundit claimed Brazil 'looked like a pub side' before Scolari's arrival, and the team's **transformation into World Cup winners** in less than 18 months is about as big a tribute to a coach's abilities as can be imagined.

Not one to rest on his laurels, Scolari stepped into the vacuum left by António Oliveira and agreed to guide Portugal through Euro 2004 – a very different job, with a very different group of players, but with a very similar objective in mind.

Russia

Vilified in Britain for the way in which they eliminated Wales from the qualifying play-offs with their former captain Yegor Titov now proven to be using performance-enhancing drugs, the Russians have a fair distance to travel to win back the admiration of Europe's football neutrals. In the eyes of their own supporters, too, there is a point to be proved. The vodka-fuelled thugs who rioted in the streets of Moscow following their team's grim display at the 2002 World Cup won't need much encouragement to repeat their protests if, as seems perfectly feasible, Russia do not progress beyond the group stage of Euro 2004.

On the other hand, the very fact that the Russians were able to triumph in the second leg in Cardiff – a game they dominated for long periods – after being cat-called off their home pitch at the end of a goalless first leg, offered a hint that the current squad has the kind of resilience so many of its predecessors have lacked. For despite their undoubted flair, too many Russian sides have failed to live up to their potential when faced with the need to compete at the highest level.

Though he has been in charge of the team for less than a year, coach Georgi Yartsev seems to have found a formula which – though it may go against the grain of Russia's often purist approach to the game – may yet allow his charges to take their proper place on the European stage.

Who they are

In the Communist era, Russia was no more and no less than the **largest republic in the Soviet Union**, and it was a team playing under the Soviet banner which competed in international competitions such as the European Championship. The Soviets won the first-ever European Nations Cup (as it was then called) in 1960, beating Yugoslavia 2–1 in the Paris final thanks to the guidance of captain Igor Netto and the inspired goalkeeping of Lev Yashin.

A gentle giant dressed all in black, Yashin would go on to become the USSR's most enduring football legend, performing regular miracles between the sticks as the team

Russia's goalscorer Vadim Evseev celebrates at the Millennium Stadium, much to the dismay of Ryan Giggs and 60,000 fans

again made it to the final in 1964, only to lose to Spain in Madrid. Following Yashin's retirement after the 1966 World Cup, the Soviets fell into decline. They were mauled 3–0 by West Germany in the 1972 Nations Cup final, and while the Soviet sides of the 1980s often played entertaining football (they again reached the European final in 1988, losing 2–0 to Holland), many of the star players were Ukrainian or Georgian rather than Russian.

As the **Soviet Union began to disintegrate**, the team competed as the CIS ('Commonwealth of Independent States') but performed abysmally at the Euro '92 finals in Sweden. At the 1994 World Cup and again at Euro '96, the team now formally known as 'Russia' in fact contained a number of Ukrainians such as the Manchester United winger Andrei Kanchelskis, who felt they had a better chance of winning honours by remaining honorary Russians rather than playing for the country of their birth. However, repeated outbreaks of in-fighting over everything from tactics to appearance fees undermined the team's ability to perform.

With the Ukraine, Baltic states such as Latvia and other former Soviet republics now established as international contenders in their own right, today's Russia is desperate to assert its **superiority over its neighbours**. Euro 2004 provides the perfect opportunity – but the omens are, to put it generously, mixed.

How they got here

The Russians scored freely in the early stages of the qualifying competition, beating Ireland 4–2 and Albania 4–1 in Moscow. They might even have been able to go into the winter break at the end of 2002 with nine points from three games, had their game in Georgia not been abandoned at half-time because of **a floodlight failure**, with the game goalless.

Come the spring, and Russia's form collapsed. The Albanians won their return fixture 3–1 in Tirana, and this was quickly followed by the rescheduled game in Tblisi, which Georgia won 1–0. The Russians then went 2–0 down away to Switzerland in Basle before Sergei Ignashevitch scored twice, the second a disputed penalty, to secure a point. The same player got the equaliser when Ireland were held 1–1 in Dublin in September 2003, but by that time **coach Valeri Gazzaev had resigned** and been replaced by Yartsev.

Feeling that Gazzaev's team selections had been overly biased towards youth, the new boss recalled a number of experienced players including Viktor Onopko, Alexander Mostovoi and Dmitri Alenichev. The blend of **old hands and new blood** in the shape of striker Dmitri Bulykin was enough to see off Switzerland (4–1) and Georgia (3–1) at home in Russia's last two group qualifiers. However, with the Swiss winning on the same day as the latter game, the Russians had to settle for runners-up spot in the group and the prospect of a two-leg play-off with Wales.

Mark Hughes' men came to Moscow to defend in the first leg, and Russia, despite enjoying 70% of possession at times, failed to translate their territorial superiority into many clear-cut chances. The second leg in Cardiff was a different story. Now able to play their more **natural counter-attacking game**, Russia scored early from a set piece and, though the Welsh dragons huffed and puffed, they rarely threatened to score the two goals they needed to keep Russia out of the finals.

How they'll play

In the short time he has been in charge, Yartsev has imposed an **unusually rigid structure** on Russia which, though the specific personnel used still vary from game to game. Barring injury or suspension, though, Sergei Ovchinnikov is the undisputed number one, having blossomed under the tutelage of a former Soviet international 'keeper, Renat Dasayev.

Ignashevitch and the veteran Onopko – now **reinstated as captain** following Titov's fall from grace – make a formidable if slightly one-paced central defensive pairing, while Vadim Evseev (Russia's goalscorer in Cardiff) and Dmitri Sennikov offer more speed in the full-back slots.

Depending on the opponents, Alexei Smertin may be used either as the midfield anchor or as an additional centre-back, allowing Onopko to move into a sweeper role. As ever, the Russians have **no shortage of would-be playmakers** – Mostovoi was disappointing against Wales and may be supplanted by the younger Vladislav Radimov or Dmitri Loskov.

Upfront, Bulykin gives Russia the kind of physical presence they have often lacked going into big tournaments, while Dmitri Sytchev and Alexander Kerzhakov are more traditional, deeper-lying forwards, their **smart running off the ball** likely to be supported from the flanks by Alenichev, Marat Izmailov or Rolan Gusev.

Who calls the shots

Like Russia's most prominent coach since the break-up of the Soviet Union, Oleg Romantsev, Georgi Yartsev **learned his trade at Spartak Moscow**. It was Romantsev who persuaded him to join Spartak's coaching staff in 1994, and Yartsev coached the team to the Russian championship two years later, after his mentor had left to take charge of the national side.

Yartsev is very much his own man, however, rejecting Romantsev's vision of a flexible, attack-orientated game plan in favour of a more disciplined approach which, so far at least, has paid Russia rich dividends.

Spain

"Defeat is unthinkable." Those were the words of Spain's star marksman Raúl González on the eve of his team's qualifying play-off against Norway. The idea that the biggest event in Europe's football calendar might take place on his country's doorstep without Spanish participation was clearly too much to bear. And it wasn't just the players who were concerned. An entire footballing nation – one of the most passionate in Europe – wanted to be sure of an invitation to the party next-door.

Now that their team's presence in the finals has been assured, thousands of Spaniards are planning to travel across the border to watch their heroes in action. Thousands more are predicted simply to turn up and take in the atmosphere, combining their love of football with a rare chance to take a convenient holiday.

If the Spaniards are likely to be among the best-supported of the 16 teams, then that backing could act as a double-edged sword. The pressure to perform – not least in the closing group encounter against Portugal themselves – will be intense, and nobody who follows the Spanish game needs reminding that the *selección* has a nasty habit of catching stage fright when the big audiences show up.

Who they are

The Spaniards have had little to celebrate in major international tournaments since they were **crowned kings of Europe** in 1964. Then, with Real Madrid and Barcelona

Not even record goalscorer Raúl seems sure which of Spain's many faces we are likely to see at Euro 2004

dominating the European club game between them, Spain hosted the final stages of the tournament and beat the Soviet Union 2–1 in the final, in front of 120,000 fans at the Chamartín stadium (today's Bernabéu).

The country failed to build on that achievement, though, and as the influence of Spain's club sides diminished during the 1970s, so the fortunes of the national side fell with it. The Spaniards even contrived to squander home advantage at the 1982 World Cup, going out at the second stage. Yet two years later, much the same side showed that they could **perform when the pressure was off**, reaching the final of the 1984 European Championship before losing 2–0 to their hosts, France.

The 1990s saw *La Liga* begin to reassert iself as one of Europe's most powerful and glamorous domestic competitions, and as playing standards rose at home, so Spain began to **promise more on the international stage**. So far, though, 'promise' rather than delivery has been the order of the day. Raúl's missed penalty proved costly at Euro 2000 as France again got the better of the Spaniards, while at the 2002 World Cup, diabolical refereeing put paid to Spanish hopes in a controversial quarter-final tie with South Korea.

As in the Premiership, many of the biggest stars in *La Liga* are foreign. Yet Spain continues to produce prodigious quantities of young talent, and Portugal – close enough to feel like home, yet without the pressure of actually being there – may just be the setting for the current team to end its long trophy drought.

How they got here

In a qualifying group that looked tricky but not insurmountable, all was going according to plan for the Spaniards until June 2003, when their traditional bugbear – an **inability to turn possession into goals** – came back to haunt them twice in the space of four days. First Greece came to Zaragoza and snatched a 1–0 win, then Northern Ireland held Spain to a goalless draw in Belfast.

The Spaniards rediscovered their goal touch in the autumn, beating Ukraine 2–1 and Armenia 4–0, but it wasn't enough to earn them top spot in the group, and when the play-off draw pitched them against Norway – stubborn opponents who have embarrassed Spain in the past – **national anxiety reached fever pitch**.

Steffen Iversen poached a goal for Norway with his team's first attack of the first leg in València, but within minutes Raúl had equalised, and a late Henning Berg own-goal gave Spain the **cushion their dominance deserved**. In the second leg in Oslo, despite freezing weather, Norway were again outplaye, with Raúl, Vicente Rodriguez and Joseba Etxebarría all scoring in a 3–0 romp.

How they'll play

The 4–4–2 formation favoured by José Antonio Camacho at the last World Cup has not been tampered with by his successor as coach, Iñaki Sáez. However, the **line-up continues to evolve**, with younger players keeping the established stars on their toes. The goalkeeper's spot is a case in point, Iker Casillas having ousted the experienced

Santiago Cañizares as first choice, though the latter continues to perform reliably whenever called upon.

Michel Salgado seems certain to start at right-back, with Carles Puyol his opposite number on the left unless Sáez decides that Puyol's height is better deployed in the centre of defence – a position Iván Helguera has already successfully been moved to from midfield. Juanito, Carlos Marchena and Raúl Bravo all featured in the qualifiers and are likely to at least be selected for the squad.

The Valéncia duo of Rubén Baraja and David Albelda seem the coach's first-choice pairing to **anchor the midfield**, with wider, more attacking roles likely to fall to Etxebarría, who seems happier than when he was used as a forward by Camacho, and another Valéncia man, Vicente. Xabi Alonso, Xavi Hernández, Javier de Pedro and the experienced Gaizka Mendieta are among those waiting in the wings, confirming Spain's considerable strength in-depth.

In attack, too, Sáez has no shortage of options. Aware that Spain are often criticised for being **over-reliant on Raúl for goals**, the coach has successfully groomed Juan Carlos Valerón as a regular strike partner who can make his own contribution, either drawing defenders away with his clever running from deep, or carving out his own space if Raúl is heavily man-marked. The likes of Guti, Fernando Morientes and Diego Tristán have all been in contention for auxiliary striking roles, but the recent emergence of two 20-year-old prodigies, Atlético Madrid's Fernando Torres and Arsenal's José António Reyes, has given everybody – not least the coach – food for thought.

Who calls the shots

Though he earned a handful of caps for his country as a player and had coached a number of clubs in the top two Spanish divisions, Iñaki Sáez did not really come to prominence until he joined the national football federation's coaching setup in 1996. Put in **overall charge of Spain's youth system** with responsibility for several levels of competition, Sáez made an immediate impact, masterminding victories in the 1998 European Under-21 Championship and the World Youth Cup a year later.

This was followed by a silver medal with an Under-20 side at the 2000 Olympic Games in Sydney, and victory in the European Under-19 Championship two years later. Then, with several of Spain's older players retiring from international duty at the same time as Camacho quit the first-team coach's job, Sáez seemed a natural choice to take over the reins.

Few doubt that Spain will bring one of the most talented squads to Portugal, or that Sáez is well-placed to find the **best of the many permutations** open to him. If he can ensure that his forwards don't suffer from the loss of confidence that briefly afflicted them during qualifying last summer, his job may already be half done.

Group B: Croatia

As usual, the rest of Europe has paid little attention to Croatia's progress toward the finals of a major international tournament. And, as usual, the lack of attention suits the Croats just fine.

Ever since they first upset the footballing *status quo* with a victory in Italy on their way to the finals of Euro '96, Croatia have revelled in their role of enigmatic underdogs. Eight years on, and while the 'Golden Generation' that brought the former Yugoslav republic a bronze medal at the 1998 World Cup may all have hung up their boots, a younger, less experienced but equally determined group of players have taken their place.

Like the previous generation, this one has the support of a wily coach who has seen it all before; combines gritty, occasionally ugly defending with breathtaking midfield craft and goal-poaching genius; and has a habit of saving its best for those rare occasions when the eyes of the world are turned in its direction. Whether this current Croat side can emulate the achievements of its predecessor will depend as much on the attitude of the opposition as on the men in the red-and-white check shirts themselves.

Who they are

Croatia was not recognised as a sovereign footballing nation until some time after the republic itself had declared independence from Yugoslavia in 1991. Even then, the international sanctions that were applied to Yugoslavia during the civil wars which raged across that region continued to apply to Croatia, preventing the young country from entering qualifying for the 1994 World Cup.

By the time the barriers to participation were finally lifted in time for Croatia to begin the qualifying phase for Euro '96, few recalled that so many of Yugoslavia's most promising players had been Croats. In fact, the **backbone of the Yugoslav team** that won the 1987 World Youth Cup was Croatian, and the Yugoslav side which began qualifying for Euro '92 – even if not the one which ended it – had a number of Croat stars playing key roles.

Even after Italy had been beaten in Palermo in 1995, the world seemed unprepared for the **sheer audacity of Croatia's football**. With Zvonimir Boban, Robert Prosinečki and Davor Šuker all relishing their first appearance on a grand stage, Turkey and Denmark were comfortably despatched in the Croats' opening two games of Euro '96. With qualification for the next phase in the bag, coach Miroslav Blažević put out what amounted to a reserve side for the last group game against Portugal, and Croatia's defeat in that game saw them pitched against Germany in the quarter-finals – an ill-tempered clash at Old Trafford which the Germans edged 2–1.

Two years later, at the 1998 World Cup, Croatia gained their revenge over Germany, winning their quarter-final 3–0. They then took the lead against France in the semis before bowing out 2–1, bouncing back to beat the Netherlands in the third-place play-off – a match which saw Šuker crowned as the tournament's top scorer.

Just as Turkey were to do four years later, Croatia followed up their world bronze with failure to qualify for Europe's showpiece finals. They returned to the international limelight – without Blažević and with the team very much in transition – at the 2002 World Cup, and though another win over Italy offered hope, the Croats' inability to beat Ecuador in their final match saw them eliminated at the group stage.

How they got here

Qualifying Group 8 was always going to be **a three-way battle** between Belgium, Bulgaria and Croatia, and in the end the margin between the three nations could scarcely have been narrower. With hindsight, two dropped points at home to Estonia in their opening fixture cost the Croats dear, as they finished a point behind Bulgaria in the final table despite beating them 1–0 in their final game. Level on points with Croatia were the Belgians, meaning that runners-up spot had to be decided on the record between the two teams. And while the Croats had lost 2–1 in Brussels toward the end of the campaign, the 4–0 home win Croatia had notched over Belgium in March 2003 proved decisive.

In the play-offs, the Croats were **drawn against their next-door neighbours** Slovenia. In the first leg in Zagreb, the Slovenes' ability to eke unfeasible results out of play-offs looked as though it would again assert itself, after Ermin Šiljak had equalised Dado Pršo's opener for Croatia. But Šiljak was suspended for the second leg in Ljubljana, and though the Croats had defender Igor Tudor red-carded on the hour, Pršo stabbed home the only goal of the game shortly afterwards, sending Croatia's substantial travelling support into raptures.

How they'll play

Throughout the former Yugoslavia, huge importance is placed on consistency of coaching at all levels **from schoolboy to full international**. While each coach has his own ideas, the basic principles of close control, keeping possession and good organisation when the opponents have the ball remain constant.

So while coach Otto Barić has introduced the odd innovation since taking charge of the national team after the 2002 World Cup, Croatia's 4–4–2 formation and general approach to the game have not been altered. Barić's most pressing concern was the Croats' defensive fragility, and the fact that first-choice 'keeper Stipe Pletikosa kept **seven clean sheets during qualifying** speaks volumes for the team's transformation since their disappointing showing in the Far East.

Juventus stopper Tudor normally marshalls the defence in front of Pletikosa, but there are doubts over his fitness. It also looks as though Barić will be unable to select Tudor's obvious partner, Liverpool's Igor Biščan, since the latter has been banned by the Croatian FA after walking out of a training camp prior to last year's qualifier against Bulgaria.

Robert Kovac and Dario Šimić are experienced players who, though nominally midfield men, could fill in at the back if required, while either of the younger full-backs, Darijo Srna and Josip Šimunić, could also conceivably be moved into a more central role.

Croatia's midfield will have **plenty of talent to parade**, albeit in not quite such a polished state as in previous tournaments. Niko Kovac and Giovani Rosso are the likely ball-winners, while Milan Rapaić, Jerko Leko and Marko Babić vie for the opportunity to fill Prosinečki's boots as the team's playmaker-in-chief.

Upfront, it was Ivica Olić who came on as a substitute to snatch victory from the jaws of defeat against Italy two years ago, but while his star has continued to rise, that of Monaco's Pršo has if anything surpassed it. The question is whether the duo can be made to **work together as a convincing partnership**, or whether, as in the case of Šuker and Alen Bokšić before them, they tend to perform

Croatia survived a bruising play-off encounter with neighbours Slovenia

better as lone strikers, with a link man – perhaps the ever-willing Ivica Mornar – providing support from a deeper role.

Who calls the shots

Though most of his accolades have been earned outside his native land, Otto Barić **needed no introduction** to Croat fans when he was appointed national-team coach in the summer of 2002. His first major honour as a coach was the Austrian *Bundesliga* title, which he won with Admira Wacker back in 1971. Since then a string of further domestic honours have come his way with teams in Austria, Germany and Croatia itself, although his only other international appointment – as Austrian national coach – ended prematurely.

Barić will be 71 by the time Euro 2004 is played, but with his own past form and that of his team, few would bet on his bowing out without a smile.

England

Consistent performers on the field of play, England come into the 2004 finals having lost just twice in competitive football since the end of Euro 2000. Yet the squad's preparations for a major tournament are in danger of being overshadowed by events off the pitch. The banning of Rio Ferdinand for failing to attend a drugs test and coach Sven Göran Eriksson's apparent reluctance to commit himself to England beyond 2006 (despite the offer of a two-year extension by his employers, the Football Association) clouded the horizon before 2004 was a month old, and it seems certain there will be other unwelcome diversions before the big kick-off in Portugal.

In this respect, the English scene is beginning to resemble that in Spain, Italy or the Netherlands – countries where football-obsessed media have always tended to exploit the tiniest hint of discord in order to sell more newspapers or pay-TV subscriptions. The number of column inches and on-air hours dedicated to the England team will hit unprecedented heights as Euro 2004 approaches, and if the players themselves are performing well on the pitch, an untold tale needs to be found on the sidelines.

When dealing with the various crises thus far, Eriksson has trodden a careful line between sympathy for his players and respect for his employers. His results deserve to speak for themselves and, if England can improve on the quarter-final place they achieved under his guidance at the last World Cup, there will be no other story worth listening to.

Who they are

England is revered the world over as being the birthplace of modern football. But while London was the home of the first football federation and the industrial towns of the north and Midlands gave birth to the first domestic league in the late nineteenth century, **the English were latecomers** to the idea of serious international competition. The FA did not send a team to the World Cup until 1950, and likewise steered clear of the fledgling European Nations Cup when it was first held a decade later. Even European club competitions were frowned upon for years.

When the English finally hosted a major tournament, the World Cup of 1966, they made up for lost time. Manager Alf Ramsey's line-up was the first England team to play 4–4–2 and it beat all-comers at Wembley – most famously West Germany, 4–2, in a final dominated by Geoff Hurst's hat-trick. The Germans got their revenge four years later when they beat England 3–2 in the quarter-finals in Mexico, and so began a long-running rivalry that would see **Germany thwart English ambitions** at virtually every turn. A penalty shoot-out win for the Germans put Bobby Robson's brave side out of the 1990 World Cup in Italy, and despite home advantage, Terry Venables' arguably more talented team met the same fate at Wembley during Euro '96. Four years later, a solitary Alan Shearer goal gave Kevin Keegan's men victory over the old enemy in Charleroi, and the English finally felt able to **bury their ghosts**. The sad fact, however, was that both England and Germany were outplayed by their group rivals, and both left Euro 2000 early. The teams that went through in their place – Portugal and Romania – may not have had undreamt of millions flowing through their domestic game, but they had dedicated an energy to tactics and youth development which their wealthier opponents lacked.

The 2002 World Cup, which saw England narrowly beaten by Brazil in the quarter-finals, showed that under Eriksson the team was beginning to combine its undoubted passion with tactical nous and a dose of **renewed self-esteem**. But if anyone thinks Euro 2004 will present England with an easier path to glory, they may be in for an unpleasant surprise.

How they got here

After England's World Cup defeat by Brazil in 2002, one pundit commented that Eriksson's players were beginning matches strongly but ending them with their backs against the wall. Whether there has been a conscious effort to reverse that trend or not, the fact remains that in qualifying for Euro 2004, England did most of their best work in the second half of matches.

Not that the new trend was without its problems. Eriksson's previously well-disciplined defence **conceded unlikely early goals** against the likes of Slovakia and Macedonia, forcing the team to come from behind to earn the points they needed to keep pace with Group 7's front-runners, Turkey. When the big games against the Turks came around, however, England rose to the occasion. In April 2003, a 2–0 home win, inspired by the 17-year-old Wayne Rooney and sealed with two goals in the last 15 minutes, put the English on top of the group table for the first time.

With no further points dropped, England knew that a draw in Istanbul in their final fixture would be enough to secure a place in Portugal. The build-up to the game was marred not by security concerns (there was no official supporters' trip to the match) but by **the threat of a boycott** by players sympathising with the now banned Ferdinand. Once the players had been persuaded to back down, however, the English again held firm, drawing 0–0 after David Beckham had spectacularly fluffed a penalty.

How they'll play

Eriksson's calm and studious attitude to the game has brought **a quiet revolution** to the way in which England approach big matches. He has abandoned the various experiments in 'modern' formations which were the undoing of his predecessors, Kevin Keegan and Glenn Hoddle, opting instead for flexibility within a standard framework of 4–4–2. His main problem has been not an inability to communicate his ideas to the players, but the continuing uncertainty as to which players are actually going to be available to him. More than any other England manager in the past, the Swede has seen his requirements shunted to the bottom of the priority pile by the Premiership's increasingly affluent and arrogant club sides who, rather than viewing international fixtures as a way of raising their industry's profile, seem to see them as an irritant at best.

It is a curious fact of Eriksson's life that players who are ruled out of friendlies because of injury often seem to show no sign of these knocks when turning out for their clubs or for competitive internationals. Despite being dogged by a long list of absentees for much of the qualifying campaign, he was able to field a **remarkably stable line-up**.

Even so, the list of first-choice players to have suffered significant injuries during the 2003/04 season makes **depressing reading**, with the attacking half of the field (Rooney, Michael Owen, Steven Gerrard *et al*) especially badly affected. At the back, too, there are concerns, with David James having replaced David Seaman as first-choice goalkeeper despite rarely showing the same consistency, and the absence of Ferdinand also having to be thrown into the equation.

Not surprisingly, Eriksson and the millions who watch England's every move have come to view David Beckham, who has made the transition from the Premiership to *La Liga* with impressive ease, as the pivotal figure around whom the rest of the team's machinery turns. Not since Paul Gascoigne has England had a player with

Inspirational to his players but troubled by the politics surrounding them, Sven Göran Eriksson has plenty to think about

the ability to inspire both with his football and his will to win – and, unlike Gazza, Beckham seems comfortable in the **media spotlight** which burns ever brighter in his and his team-mates' eyes.

Who calls the shots

Though it seems hard to believe now, the FA was lambasted in sections of the English media for appointing Sven Göran Eriksson after Kevin Keegan resigned following a 1-0 home defeat by Germany in October 2000. How would the players respond to being coached by a foreigner? What interest could he possibly have in England's success? And what about all the other eminently qualified Englishmen who had been passed over in preference to the Swede?

When England won their return World Cup qualifier against Germany 5–1 in Munich in September 2001, even Eriksson's most xenophobic critics were silenced. Many have since returned to **haunt and taunt him** but, thanks to a long career which has taken him to a range of different situations in a variety of different countries, the coach always seems to have the right way of responding to them.

Like a number of top coaches, Eriksson enjoyed only a brief playing career before long-term injury forced him to hang up his boots and find an alternative means of **staying in football**. His IFK Gothenburg side became the first Swedish team to win a European trophy with victory in the UEFA Cup in 1982, and Eriksson was to come within one game of the continent's highest accolade, the European Cup, with the Portuguese club Benfica in 1990.

His *Serie A* experience included spells at AS Roma and Fiorentina, and in 2000 he guided Lazio to their first European honour, the Cup-Winners' Cup. Twelve months later Lazio won the *Serie A* title but, by the time the *scudetto* was adorning their shirts, Eriksson had already taken up his first international post in London...

France

Like a scratch across the bonnet of a vintage Bugatti racer, France's first-round exit from the 2002 World Cup continues to blight perceptions of what is still arguably the greatest national football team on the planet. Since they bowed out from that tournament after failing to score in any of their three matches, the French have all won all but one of their competitive games, being crowned winners of the Confederations Cup and qualifying for Euro 2004 without dropping a point. Yet still that blemish on their record remains to sow the seeds of doubt in the psyche of France's football public. They failed in the Far East – could they fail again in Portugal?

Jacques Santini is not taking any chances. Since taking over as first-team coac from Roger Lemerre following the World Cup disaster, Santini has given the squad *carte blanche* to attack whenever the opportunity arises. His team selections have been more aggressive; his tactics more ambitious. The results have spoken for themselves, and the players, too, seem happier.

Rarely has the rallying cry of *Allez les Bleus!* seemed more appropriate than now, as the French travel to Portugal confident of mouting a better defence of their European title than they managed of the World Cup two years ago. You might get good odds against history repeating itself and France making another first-round exit; you'd be mad to take them.

Who they are

It was the French who gave the world the idea of competitive international football. The World Cup was the brainchild of Jules Rimet, who had the first trophy named after him; Gabriel Hanot dreamt up the European Cup for club sides; while another Frenchman, Henri Delaunay, came up with the concept of the European Nations Cup – as a result, the **European Championship trophy** now bears his name.

Strangely, though, it was a while before France's footballers made much of an impact on the competitions their fellow countrymen had devised. In fact, the French did not threaten to win anything until they hosted the European Championship of 1984. A **classic attacking midfield** containing Jean Tigana, Alain Giresse and skipper Michel Platini beat Portugal 3–2 in an epic semi-final in Marseilles, then beat Spain 2–0 in a more prosaic final in Paris to bring Delaunay's trophy home for the first time.

Platini went on to become coach of the national side and led France to the Euro '92 finals in Sweden, where the attacking duo of Jean-Pierre Papin and Eric Cantona made them one of the **pre-tournament favourites**. Yet, just as they would do ten years later at the World Cup, the French flattered to deceive – they failed to win a group game, and Platini resigned.

Six years later, with the World Cup being played in their own backyard, it was a lack of natural goalscorers that was supposed to stand in France's way. It didn't bother them: with **near-perfect defensive organisation** and playmaker Zinedine Zidane emerging as an all-time great, the hosts powered their way into the final where they beat a strangely muted Brazil, 3–0.

No country had ever won the European Championship while being World Cup holders, but at Euro 2000 the French showed they were **no respecters of precedent**. They came from behind to beat Portugal in the semi-finals, then broke Italian hearts with a last-minute equaliser and extra-time winner at the final in Rotterdam.

How they got here

The sceptics who claim the current French side is not as complete as the Class of 2000 point eagerly to the qualifying draw for 2004, which pitched *les Bleus* against Slovenia, Israel, Cyprus and Malta. True enough, it was **hardly the toughest of tests**, and once the Slovenes – arguably the toughest of the quartet – had been mauled

5–0 in Paris in France's first home fixture, the path to the finals rarely looked like being blocked for long. By any measure, though, the nature of the team's progress was still impressive: the French scored 29 goals and conceded just two in their eight matches, and they were the only side in all ten groups to finish with a 100% record.

Equally worthy of praise was the way in which Santini's side, most of whom play in the high-pressure leagues of England and Italy, managed to brush worries about long fixture-lists to one side to **lift the Confederations Cup** in the summer of 2003. At a time when most of their European rivals were already on holiday, the French were adding to their silverware collection, playing five ties against world-class opposition and winning every one of them...

With Henry on song, France can no longer complain of lacking a natural goalscorer

How they'll play

If Santini's plan was to make the French more attack-minded after the goal drought of 2002, then it has been brought to realisation partly through the maturing of two players, Thierry Henry and David Trezeguet, into strikers with a **real killer instinct**. The coach's preference now is to use the duo as a genuine attacking partnership, rather than to give Henry a roving role behind the frontline as Lemerre preferred. Not only has the switch brought goals, it has also encouraged other French strikers to stake a claim – notably Louis Saha, Steve Marlet and Péguy Luyindula.

In midfield, too, competition for places is fierce, despite the international retirement of Olivier Deschamps and Youri Djorkaeff. Zidane is still the clear favourite to **pull the creative strings** from a central position, with the Arsenal duo of

Robert Pires and Sylvain Wiltord giving him the option of spreading the play to either flank. Behind him, Patrick Viera, Olivier Dacourt and Claude Makelele vie for attention as anchorman-in-waiting.

At the back, Marcel Desailly is by no means assured of a place despite regularly captaining the team when he is selected. Lilian Thuram has shown he can make the transition from full-back to centre-back, allowing Bixente Lizarazu and Mikaël Silvestre to claim **wider defensive roles** for themselves – although the Auxerre pairing of Philippe Mexès and Jean-Alain Boumsong, who came to prominence in last year's Confederations Cup, may have something to say about that.

Who calls the shots

Like the great Platini, Jacques Santini first made his name as a player with the Saint-Étienne side which **dominated French football** in the mid-1970s. He has also coached the club, but did not really come to prominence until he took charge of Olympique Lyonnais in 2000. Despite being one of France's best-resourced teams, Lyon had never won the domestic title until Santini's emphasis on attack brought them the championship in 2002.

After that triumph Santini was made director of football by Lyon, but within months the French FA came calling to offer him the job of national-team coach. Roger Lemerre had resigned after France's **catastrophic showing** at the World Cup finals that summer, but although morale within the national setup was at a low ebb, Santini did not hesitate to accept the offer. And, so far at least, Santini's results suggest he did the right thing.

Switzerland

With all due respect to the nation's famous clock and watch industry, Switzerland's qualification for Portugal could not have been better timed. The success of the national team promises to breathe fresh life into the Swiss domestic game, which in the last couple of years has seen a string of big clubs hit money troubles and some names disappear altogether. Similarly, UEFA's controversial decision to award the next European finals (in 2008) jointly to Austria and Switzerland has been made to look more astute by the latter's success.

Whether the Swiss have what it takes to make further progress is another matter. Coach Jakob 'Köbi' Kuhn worked wonders with a limited squad to lead Switzerland to the top of their qualifying group, and enjoys a rapport with the side which few coaches have managed in recent years. Injuries permitting, he should also be able to pick a settled team, with most of the players who starred in the qualifiers likely to travel to Portugal.

Ultimately, though, the Swiss played well above themselves even to get this far. Kuhn has little in the way of extra resources to call on if his first choices are not available for selection, and while the Swiss do have young talent coming through (they were crowned European Under-17 champions in 2002), it looks a better bet for Euro 2008 than 2004.

Who they are

Switzerland was one of the first nations in mainland Europe to embrace football, after the game was brought to the country by British expats in the mid-19th century. Today Switzerland hosts the headquarters of Euro 2004 organisers UEFA (in Nyon, on the shores of Lake Geneva) and of world football's governing body FIFA (in Zürich). Yet for all its **history and prestige**, not to mention material wealth, the country has produced little in the way of great footballing talent.

Even when they hosted the World Cup in 1954, the Swiss contrived to squander their advantage, losing 7–5 to Austria in **a bizarre quarter-final** that had seen them race into a 3–0 lead. It was to be 40 years before the nation made a similar impact. A former Crystal Palace player and journeyman European coach by the name of Roy Hodgson guided Switzerland to the second round of the 1994 World Cup in the USA. The team included some of the finest attacking talent the country has every produced, including strikers Alain Sutter and Stéphane Chapuisat, and playmaker Ciriaco Sforza.

Much the same side also qualified for Euro '96 – Switzerland's first appearance in the European Championship finals. But by the time the Swiss kicked-off the tournament's opener against England at Wembley, **Hodgson had been dismissed** by the Swiss FA for trying to combine his job with that of first-team coach at Inter Milan. His replacement, Artur Jorge, imposed his own ideas on the team but failed to engender the same dedication from the squad. The Swiss left England after finishing bottom of their group.

How they got here

The Swiss were widely viewed as being likely third-place finishers when they were drawn in a qualifying group containing Ireland and Russia – both of whom had made it to the 2002 World Cup. But Swiss coach Köbi Kuhn had a few tricks up his sleeve. His team's **crafty, counter-attacking style** was perfectly blended to tame Irish exuberance and frustrate Russian guile. Fabio Celestini's late goal stunned the Dublin crowd and earned Switzerland a 2–1 win in October 2002, while at home to Russia the following June, the Swiss raced into a two-goal lead with a brace from Alexander Frei. The Russians clawed their way back to claim a draw, and Ricardo Cabanas' dismissal in the return game was the cue for Switzerland to go down to their only defeat of the campaign – a 4–1 drubbing in Moscow.

Despite that result, the Swiss were still top of the group going into their final game at home to the Irish in Basle. The 38,000 crowd packed inside the new St

Brotherly love: Hakan (left) and Murat Yakin typify the spirit that has taken Switzerland to the finals

Jakob stadium knew that a win would take their team to Portugal, and their nerves were settled after six minutes when Hakan Yakin rounded Shay Given to score after Frei's shot was half-blocked by the Irish defence. Ireland, needing a win to keep their hopes of qualification alive, poured forward but could not find an equaliser. Instead, Frei prodded home on the hour after Chapusiat's header was parried by Given, and the Swiss, having **ridden their luck** a little, were through.

How they'll play

Coach Kuhn became more cautious as the qualifying campaign went on, having been alarmed by the way his defence crumbled in Moscow. Even so, he has tended to resist the temptation to pack his midfield as some Swiss coaches have done in the past. Instead, he allows key man Hakan Yakin **a roving role** behind the two front players, knowing that the player has a good enough engine to track back when needed. Yakin's ability to draw markers away from his fellow strikers has been good news for Frei and the veteran Chapuisat, still his first-choice partner in attack despite the fact that he will be nudging 35 by the time of the finals. If 'Chapi' tires in Portugal, the younger legs of Léonard Thurre or Marco Streller will be capable if largely untried replacements.

Though Yakin influences midfield, he does not dominate it. One of Switzerland's most consistent performers in qualifying was the playmaker Raphael Wicky, whose ability to **spread the play quickly** comes in useful to a team which, Chapuisat aside, has plenty of pace about it. Also influential is the younger, more temperamental Cabanas, who recently returned to Grasshopper Zürich after an unhappy six-month spell in French football.

Johann Vogel generally takes **the anchorman role**, playing just in front of a back four which has Hakan Yakin's elder brother, Murat, at its fulcrum. The choice as to who partners Yakin is a toss-up between Stéphane Henchoz and Patrick Müller – the latter has been in better form for his country but, like Cabanas, has been struggling to get first-team football in France.

Regardless of who and how they play, it seems certain that Switzerland will need their goalkeepers to be on top form in Portugal. Luckily they have at least two at the **peak of their powers** – the extrovert Pascal Zuberbühler and the calmer veteran Jörg Stiel.

Who calls the shots

Switzerland's arrival as an international force during the 1990s was prompted by foreign coaches – notably Roy Hodgson and his immediate predecessor, German-born Uli Stielike. Which is why, for so long, the Swiss FA pursued a policy of **appointing only foreigners** to the role, even though there were arguably better candidates at home.

There was uproar when, in 2000, the FA refused to give the job to Swiss-born Hans-Peter Zaugg despite his impressive run as caretaker boss, awarding it instead to an Argentinian, Enzo Trossero. And it was Trossero's failure to get Switzerland even as far as a play-off spot for the 2002 World Cup – after a campaign that included a home defeat by Slovenia – that finally led the FA in the direction of Köbi Kuhn.

Capped more than 60 times by his country as a player, Kuhn garnered success and respect in equal measure as coach of Switzerland's Under-17 and Under-21 sides. Since taking charge of the full team in summer 2001, Kuhn has proved once and for all that the Swiss can coach at least as well as they can play. His reward has been a contract extension until the end of next year.

Group C: Bulgaria

There is a school of thought in the Bulgarian media that their team would have been better off not qualifying for Euro 2004. Plamen Markov's side will be one of the youngest in Portugal, and some critics worry openly that if the team suffers a couple of heavy defeats in the finals, it will undermine their prospects for the next World Cup.

It's a sentiment that few on the terraces share. After the disintegration of the great Bulgarian team that reached the semi-finals of USA '94, the country's football infrastructure all but collapsed. Young stars left for foreign leagues before so much as staking a regular first-team place at home, and even top clubs such as Levski Sofia were obliged to let supporters into games for free because they couldn't afford to employ anyone to man the turnstiles. The fortunes of the national side plumbed new depths when a 6–0 crushing by the Czech Republic ended hopes of qualifying for the 2002 World Cup.

The national side's rapid bounce back to form has surprised many both inside and outside Bulgaria, not least after the last links with the Class of '94 were severed by the international retirement of Krasimir Balakov and Radostin Kishishev during the Euro 2004 qualifying campaign. The young-sters called up to fill their shoes have done their country proud – and given the domestic game a much-needed shot in the arm. Even if the predictions of doom come true and the Bulgarians go no further than the first round in Portugal, the momentum toward renewal will be hard to stop.

Who they are

Before 1994, Bulgaria had never won a match in the finals of a major tournament. The man who helped change that more than any other was Hristo Stoichkov, a hot-tempered forward who combined a **formidable physique** with an exquisite touch, a sprinter's acceleration and the leadership qualities of a born captain. After the fall of Communism in the Eastern Bloc, Stoichkov and his contemporaries – men like the wily playmaker Balakov, extrovert defender Trifon Ivanov and energetic midfielder Yordan Lechkov – had moved to big West European clubs, giving them a competitive edge which previous Bulgarian teams had lacked.

In the US, Stoichkov's team overcame a defeat by Nigeria in their opening game, beating Greece, Argentina, Mexico and, most memorably, Germany 2–1 to reach the semi-finals. Had the Bulgarians been awarded the second penalty TV replays showed they should have been given against Italy, they might even have swaggered into the final itself. As it was, fourth place wasn't a bad return for a team with so little in the way of international pedigree.

Unlike their neighbours in Romania, Bulgaria's team faded fast. Many of Stoichkov's generation – even the great man himself – were past their prime by the time Euro '96 came along, and the Bulgars left England after the first round.

After a similar group-stage exit from the 1998 World Cup, Stoichkov hung up his boots and the fortunes of the national team went into freefall. As Stoichkov himself put it, Bulgaria's fresh talent was **leaving the country too early**, depriving the nation of a footballing future by signing up for deals with minor clubs in Greece or Turkey in their eagerness to escape economic torment at home.

But what goes around comes around, and the attitude of today's Bulgarian side reflects a growing optimism in the country itself. The team are looking to the future with a mixture of excitement and apprehension – but at least they have a future to look forward to.

Stilian Petrov led by example through the Bulgars' qualifying campaign

How they got here

Group 8's three-way battle for supremacy was one of the most absorbing of the qualifying programme, with Bulgaria's young side evenly matched against Belgium and Croatia. The Bulgarians began as they meant to go on, however, winning 2–0 in Brussels with a **near-perfect display** of counter-attacking football in September 2002. They then beat Croatia by the same score in Sofia, a game notable for the interplay between Dimitar Berbatov and Stilian Petrov, who tormented the Croats with their elegant, one-touch football.

Balakov's retirement at the end of the 2002/03 season coincided with a slight hiccup. Estonian goalkeeper Mart Poom frustrated Bulgaria during a goalless draw in Tallinn, and Belgium took the lead twice in Sofia, only to be hauled back on both occasions with Berbatov again **the telling influence**.

That draw meant Bulgaria needed only to beat Estonia at home and Andorra away to seal top spot in the group – something they achieved with a bit to spare. They could even afford to lose their final qualifier in Croatia, though the nation's media were unhappy that their team had not managed to preserve its unbeaten record and had ended its campaign on a low note after a 1–0 defeat in Zagreb.

How they'll play

Few in Bulgaria will pretend that the current side has quite the panache of its predecessor of a decade ago. Coach Plamen Markov has **built confidence** from the back, where experienced 'keeper Zdravko Zdravkov enjoyed an excellent qualifying campaign, and central defenders Rosen Kirilov and Predrag Pazin have been in fine form for both club and country. Kishishev's retirement has made the right-back role more problematical, but Markov may continue his experiment with the reliable midfielder Daniel Borimirov in that position if the player can regain his fitness in the latter half of the season. The other option is Martin Stankov, who may be needed to switch sides if first-choice left-back Ivailo Petkov is out of sorts.

Markov likes his midfield to **close down the opposition** with more vigour than is the norm for teams from the Balkans. The ploy certainly seemed to work in the qualifiers, when the Bulgarians' work rate caught many of their opponents flat-footed. Kaiserslautern's Marian Hristov and Dynamo Kiev's Georgi Peev are the two lynchpins, while Stilian Petrov has taken on Balakov's mantle as the team's creative powerhouse, as well as the captain's armband.

Martin Petrov (no relation to Stilian) is flexible enough to play either in midfield or as an auxiliary striker, and may be called upon to play a roving role if, as sometimes happened in qualifying, Bulgaria appear to lack pace, width or both. Upfront, Berbatov is the obvious choice to lead the line, despite his apparent **clumsiness at times**. If fit, Svetoslav Todorov could make a useful foil, but after an injury-hit season he will have to fight hard for a place against competition from Zoran Jankovic and Vladimir Manchev, who both impressed in qualifying.

Who calls the shots

The Bulgarians went back to their footballing roots when they appointed Plamen Markov to succeed Stoicho Mladenov as national-team coach in December 2001. Markov's achievements as a coach in his native land were relatively modest – at the time of his appointment he was in charge of his hometown club, second-division Vidima-Rakovski Sevlievo.

In retrospect, Markov was chosen for **all the right reasons**. His role as playmaker in the CSKA Sofia side which reached the semi-finals of the European Cup in 1982 was one of the few bright points in Bulgaria's pre-1994 footballing history, and his 34 caps for his country included an appearance at the 1986 World Cup in Mexico.

As player-coach at the French lower-division club Grenoble, Markov had been a mentor to the young Youri Djorkaeff – the first of many such relationships which bear testimony to his ability not just to spot young talent, but to nurture it.

Plenty of other candidates for the job boasted longer lists of top honours but, as Markov proved in getting his young Bulgaria side into the finals, at international level coaching is as much about **future relationships** as it is about past achievements.

Denmark

The Danes go into Euro 2004 with a side much-changed from the one that succumbed meekly to England in the second round of the last World Cup, but one which, strangely, has many of the same assets and problems. The squad Morten Olsen takes to Portugal will be compact and confident, boasting prolific goalscorers at one end of the pitch and a towering, reliable goalkeeper at the other. Just as in 2002, however, doubts remain about the side's defensive solidity under pressure, and in the ability of Danish legs to stand the pace of an intense fixture programme in mid-summer heat.

If history does repeat itself for Denmark, then nobody should blame Olsen and his staff, who are doing everything they can to avoid a repeat performance. The coach's canny team selections stood the Danes in fine stead during qualifying, when they finished top of one of the campaign's trickiest groups. And since Denmark's place in the finals was assured, Olsen and his assistant Keld Bordinggård have recruited two Danish assistants with coaching and medical experience in the *Serie A*, where the science of sports fitness has been turned into a fine art and where, of course, they will have gained inside information on one of Denmark's Group C opponents, Italy.

Injuries and suspensions permitting, there is no reason why the Danes should not make a bigger impact on Euro 2004 than they did at the World Cup. They may not have quite the flair of some of the classic teams Olsen himself graced in an earlier era, but on the other hand, they will be far, far better prepared for the task ahead.

Who they are

In common with much of Scandinavia, football in Denmark was viewed as very much **an amateur pursuit** until well after World War II. In fact, the Danish FA did not allow professional players to represent their country until 1976. More than anyone, it was talented forward Allan Simonsen, who was crowned European Footballer of the Year in 1977, who persuaded the authorities to alter their policy. A string of other stars soon emerged, and in 1983 Denmark beat England at Wembley

Jesper Grønkjær ignores the taunts of unhappy Norway fans after scoring the only goal of the game in Copenhagen, June 2003

to qualify for the European Championship the following year. German coach Sepp Piontek's team, who would soon be dubbed 'Danish Dynamite' by their colourful and irrepressibly good-natured travelling support, made it all the way to the semi-finals in France, playing some thrilling football along the way and only losing out to Spain on penalties.

The Spaniards would again be Denmark's nemesis at the 1986 World Cup, where a team starring Morten Olsen, Preben Elkjær and Michael Laudrup went to sleep during their second-round tie after cruising through the groups with elegant ease.

By now the Danes were prodigious exporters of football talent, and nowhere was more receptive to the country's imports than England, where players such as midfielder Jan Mølby and goalkeeper Peter Schmeichel became **local folk heroes** almost overnight. At the same time, the national team's progress was stuttering – Denmark were eliminated from the qualifying stages of the 1992 European Championship by Yugoslavia. Many of the Danish players were already on their summer holidays when UEFA announced that Yugoslavia were to be banned from the tournament as a result of sanctions applied during the country's civil war, and that Denmark were to be invited to take their place. Michael Laudrup declined the invite, but his younger brother Brian, together with Schmeichel, Kim Vilfort, Flemming Povlsen and others, were happy to **put their sun-block away** and head for Sweden.

Inevitably, the team were poorly prepared and almost totally lacking match fitness. Yet they improved as the tournament went on, beating France to qualify for the knockout stage, then edging out holders Holland on penalties. In the final, Germany were out-muscled and out-thought despite enjoying the bulk of possession. Denmark won 2–0 and lifted their first major trophy – at the end of a tournament they hadn't originally qualified for.

Since then, fortune has not been quite so kind to the Danes. At the 1998 World Cup, the Laudrups' last big tournament, they were unlucky to go out 3–2 to Brazil in the quarter-finals. At Euro 2000 they were drawn in the 'group of death' and went home **without scoring a goal**. At the 2002 World Cup they again eliminated France, but were no match for an exuberant England in the second round.

Perhaps, if Morten Olsen really wants to be sure his players will stay the course in Portugal, he should send them on holiday first?

How they got here

Denmark could scarcely been given a tougher qualifying draw. Group 2 contained an uncompromising Norway side that would relish the chance to take on the Danes in a local derby; a flamboyant Romania keen to put World Cup disappointment behind it; and a maturing Bosnia-Herzegovina capable of making the young country's best-ever showing in a qualifying tournament.

Partly because it was so competitive and partly because it contained teams with such disparate playing styles, the group threw up some unpredictable results. Morten Olsen's side were held 2–2 by Norway in Oslo after the home side's John Carew nodded in a stoppage-time equaliser, comfortably beat Luxembourg 2–0 at home, then won 5–2 in Romania with the help of a sandy pitch, a 45-metre lob by Thomas Gravesen and a **bizarre own-goal** by Cosmin Contra.

Denmark were sitting pretty at the top of the group table, but a stunning 2–0 win by an inspired Bosnia in Copenhagen brought them back to reality, with Olsen admitting he had got his team selection wrong. A 1–0 win over Norway, thanks to Jesper Grønkjær's early near-post strike, put the Danes back on track, and when Martin Laursen grabbed a stoppage-time equaliser to earn a 2–2 draw at home to the revived Romanians, Denmark's fate was back in their own hands.

They now needed only a draw in their last game away to Bosnia, who in turn needed a win to top the group. The Sarajevo crowd **roared its heart out** and the Danes rode their luck – but a 1–1 draw was no less than Olsen's men deserved.

How they'll play

With a coach who is a firm believer in the 'take each game as it comes' school of management, Denmark adopt a **variety of formations** to suit their opposition. Striker Jon Dahl Tomasson has been known to operate as a lone striker, as one of a pair or at the centre of a line of three, while the midfield can feature anything between three and five players. However, the **backbone running down the middle** of the team varies surprisingly little, with Tomasson leading the line, Claus Jensen as midfield playmaker, the versatile Thomas Helveg at the centre of defence, and the reliable Thomas Sørensen between the sticks.

Elsewhere, Denmark's other first-choice forward positions are very much up for grabs, with the experienced Ebbe Sand facing stiff competition from Martin Jørgensen and the emerging Peter Løvenkrands. Pace and fitness are important here, since Olsen likes his team to counter-attack quickly and the power of Denmark's wide players, Grønkjær and Dennis Rommedahl, cries out to be exploited in the opposition penalty area.

Other selections may depend on the nature of the task in hand. Gravesen may be preferred to either Rommedahl or Grønkjær if ball-winning is the order of the day, for example, while Olsen is also looking at relatively untried defenders such as Brian Priske and Per Krøldrup to bolster a sometimes shaky-looking backline.

Who calls the shots

Holder of the Danish record for international caps until Peter Schmeichel surpassed it, Morten Olsen has been part of his country's modern football scene for as long as the scene itself has existed. He made his first appearance as a central defender for Denmark in 1970 and did not hang up his boots until 1989, with 102 caps to his name. As a club player he enjoyed success in Belgium with Anderlecht and in the *Bundesliga* with Cologne, but he returned to Denmark to **earn his coaching stripes** with Brøndby.

Feeling the need for more formal training in his new job, Olsen left for Germany to earn the DFB's coaching qualification and subsequently became head coach at Cologne and at Ajax of Amsterdam. However, his relative lack of success at that level made him by no means the natural choice to succeed Swedish-born Bo Johansson after Denmark had ended their Euro 2000 campaign without scoring a goal.

Initially, Olsen was assisted by his former international team-mate Michael Laudrup, and the pair guided Denmark as far as the second round of the 2002 World Cup. Since then Laudrup has gone his own way, but there are no indications that Olsen is tiring of the game that has been **part of his life** for so long.

Italy

Four years ago, the *Azzurri* travelled to Euro 2000 having been written off by their own media as virtual no-hopers. They reached the final and, had it not been for some unusually profligate finishing by Alessandro del Piero, would have been crowned champions of Europe for the first time in more than 30 years. Today the scenario could scarcely be more different. Italy's press are convinced that 2004 is going to be their year, and the pressure on Giovanni Trapattoni's squad will be intense.

The question is whether the players are really worth all the acclaim or whether, as has happened to Italian sides all too often in the past, the media pressure will become too much and something, somewhere will snap. Certainly, the current side has a better balance to it than that of 2000, which was very much a team in transition. Trapattoni is a more cautious coach than his predecessor, but that in itself may be to Italy's benefit – though it was the team's inability to finish off opponents, together with some atrocious officiating, which prevented the men in blue from going further than the second round of the 2002 World Cup.

As 'Trap' himself points out, gone are the days when a single team can dominate a top-level competition like the European Championship. The tournaments themselves are too long, the number of credible teams too high. What a side can do, the Italy coach believes, is play adventurous football when it can, but leave nothing to chance when the heat is really on. It's a formula which may just work in Portugal.

Who they are

Thanks mainly to the vision of Vittorio Pozzo, who created the nation's domestic league and brought new ideas about tactics and preparation to the national team during his tenure as coach between the wars, Italy became an early member of **Europe's footballing elite**. The country was the first in Europe to host the World Cup, in 1934, and Pozzo's team swept all before them. Four years later in France, and with his star forward Giuseppe Meazza now partnered by the equally talented Silvio Piola, Pozzo fashioned a successful defence of the title.

In the early postwar period, Italian clubs flourished on the new European stage but the national team's fortunes declined. The low point was reached at the 1966 World Cup, when Italy were knocked out by North Korea and the players were famously **pelted with rotten tomatoes** when they returned home. Just two years later, with foreign players now banned from the *Serie A* in an effort to nurture more homegrown talent, the Italians hosted the final stages of the European Nations Cup. Playing their own brand of counter-attacking football known as *catenaccio*, a team shaped by the midfield genius of Gianni Rivera and Sandro Mazzola beat Yugoslavia in a replayed final to take the trophy.

The Italians were to host the finals again 12 years later, though by this time the tournament had been extended to eight teams and renamed the European Championship. On their home patch, Enzo Bearzot's side were again favourites to win, but the strange structure of that year's competition saw them eliminated without losing a match. (Ironically, much the same side would progress through the first round of the World Cup two years later without winning one – and go on to lift the trophy.)

Since then it has been a case of 'so near, yet so far' for the *Azzurri*, whose record of being knocked out of tournaments on penalties rivals that of England. At Euro 2000, at least, Zoff's team **turned the tide** by winning their semi-final shoot-out against the Netherlands – then came within a whisker of winning the final in normal time.

How they got here

The turning point in Italy's qualifying campaign came on 6 September 2003, when after an hour gone in their home game against Wales, Pippo Inzaghi finally broke the deadlock from close range. The goal did more than break Welsh resistance; it opened the floodgates for a 4–0 win (Inzaghi bagged a hat-trick) that gave Trapattoni's team the confidence they'd lacked until that point.

The win over Wales was also **sweet revenge** for the 2–1 defeat Mark Hughes' side had inflicted on the Italians in Cardiff the previous October – a result which, along with some other impressive Welsh displays, looked as though it might consign Italy to runners-up spot in the group, and the uncertainty of the play-offs.

Even after the defeat of Wales, Italy's progress wasn't perfect. They were held to a 1–1 draw in Belgrade by a surprisingly strong Serbia & Montenegro side, but it didn't matter, since the Welsh themselves were by now dropping points as if they were going out of fashion. A 4–0 demolition of Azerbaijan in Reggio Calabria in their final match was enough to see the *Azzurri* through.

How they'll play

"Never leave the result to chance," is their coach's motto, and in the circumstances it would be silly to expect the Italians, with a conservative coach and a long tradition of **defence-minded football**, to approach Euro 2004 with all guns blazing. That said, Trapattoni is not afraid to present an attacking formation when the situation demands it – as he did for the decisive home qualifier against Wales, when Italy needed a win and Italy lined up with an untypical three-man frontline.

Ordinarily, though, the Italians line up as either a 4–4–2 or a 4–5–1, with Christian Vieri the favourite for the lone striker's role if the latter formation is used, and Inzaghi and Antonio Cassano among Vieri's possible partners in the former line-up – though both have had **injury-disrupted seasons** in 2003/04. Del Piero's versatility means he can play either in a line of three or as the most advanced midfield player, tucked in behind the frontline.

For Trapattoni, though, the key man is playmaker Francesco Totti who, despite having had a poor World Cup two years ago, is now reckoned to be mature enough to make Euro 2004 the stage for his unique talents. Whether he can rise to the occasion remains to be seen, of course, but Italy certainly need him to, for they without him they are short of both pace and vision in the centre of the park.

Fortunately, given Totti's inability to prove himself at this level so far, Stefano Fiore may be poised for a return to favour. Fiore was the unsung hero of Italy's Euro 2000 campaign, ensuring that Italy's often meagre morsels of possession were put to good

The turning point – Pippo Inzaghi completes his hat hat-trick in the home qualifier against Wales

use, but has endured a couple of barren years at club level which have hindered his international progress.

The holding roles in midfield pose fewer problems, in as much as Trapattoni has both a **regular favoured combination** – Chrisian Zanetti and Simone Perrotta – and plenty of cover for them. Andrea Pirlò, Gennaro Gattuso, Mauro Camoranesi and Alessio Tacchinardi are all proven ball-winners, even if their coach would rather they had sufficient pace to enable Italy to use more of the width of the pitch.

Oddly, given the team's heritage, the Italians lack the same kind of cover in defence, where Alessandro Nesta and Fabio Cannavaro have been such a constant at the heart of things that few other players have been able to get a look-in. Nicola Legrottaglie is one player who could conceivably fill either role should one of Trap's first choices be injured, while left-back Gianluca Zambrotta is capable of switching inside. At right-back, Massimo Oddo made a huge difference when he was brought on to replace Christian Pannucci in the key qualifier at home to Wales, and with Italy needing their **full-backs to attack** more often these days, he has every right to expect a starting role.

The Italians went 524 minutes in qualifying without conceding a goal and, as well as the backline, the form of goalkeeper Gianluigi Buffon has alaso been critical. Buffon missed the last World Cup when he broke his hand on the eve of the tournament, so will be keen to impress at this level. Christian Abbiati stands by in case Buffon makes a return journey to A&E.

Who calls the shots

The one great mystery surrounding Giovanni Trapattoni is that it took him so long to become coach of Italy. The country's **most successful club coach** of the modern era, 'Trap' has been there at every stage of the Italian game's recent evolution.

As a player he was part of the AC Milan team that first challenged Spanish domination of the European Cup in the 1960s. As a coach, he created the brilliant Juventus side which won five *Serie A* titles and a string of European honours in the late 1970s and early '80s. He then moved on to Inter and was the last coach to lead 'the other Milan' to the Italian championship.

The only blot on his copybook has been an unhappy spell at Bayern Munich in the mid-1990s, where his incoherent ramblings in pidgin German were sampled and turned into a **hip-hop record**. Trap had already returned to Italy – and in fact had just resigned as coach of a near-bankrupt Fiorentina – when his predecessor Dino Zoff was hounded out of his job by public criticism of his 'failure' to get Italy past the French in the final of Euro 2000…

Sweden

Unconventional to the last, the Swedes approach Euro 2004 still not knowing if they can tempt their most prolific goalscorer out of international retirement for a second time, with their joint coaches having agreed to an amicable divorce (but not until the tournament has finished), and with about half their first-choice team unable to get a game for their clubs.

For the about-to-separate coaching couple of Lars Lagerbäck (staying) and Tommy Söderberg (going), qualifying for Portugal has been the easy bit. Sweden survived a loss of form by goalkeeper Magnus Hedman and the second 'retirement' of his club colleague at Celtic, striker Henrik Larsson, winning their group so comfortably that they were able to lose their last match at home to Latvia without jepoardising their position.

Now comes the task of raising Sweden's game sufficiently for them to perform well repeatedly in the space of a few days and against top-level opponents – something the nation's best players have not managed since the World Cup of 1994.

Who they are

Unlike their near-neighbours and Group C rivals Denmark, the Swedes hold their domestic football season over the summer. The tradition dates back to 1959, when the Swedish FA decided to try to capitalise on the interest in football generated by the country's hosting of the World Cup the previous year. Then, a mixed bag of local amateurs and experienced professionals who **returned from exile** in Italy surprised everybody by reaching the final, where their crude, physical football was no match for the brilliance of Brazil, and they were crushed 5–2.

In the short term, the summer season was a failure – vast crowds did not come flocking to watch Djurgårdens entertain Malmö in 1959. But as the years have gone by, fielding players who are relatively fresh has enabled Sweden to **stay the course** of big tournaments more consistently than Denmark.

In 1974 the Swedes reached the second group phase of the World Cup, taking the lead against the hosts and eventual winners West Germany before eventually going down 4–2. When Sweden hosted the European Championship finals in 1992, Tommy Svensson's side strolled past Denmark, England and France before again losing to the Germans at the semi-final stage. Two years later, they reached the semi-finals of the World Cup where they were a little unlucky to lose 1–0 to Brazil.

Since then, the Swedes have tended to under-perform on the big stage. The purists back home would say this is because so many Swedish stars now play in the 'winter' leagues of southern and western Europe, and they may have a point. Despite **qualifying with aplomb**, Sweden left Euro 2000 without winning a match, after Larsson, big striker Kennet Andersson and influential midfielder Stefan Schwarz had all either played through the pain of long-term injuries or failed to make it onto the pitch at all.

A unique team spirit, rather than outstanding individualism, has propelled Sweden into the finals

How they got here

Sweden's lack of natural goalscoring prowess looked initially as though it would stand between them and the finals. They were held 0–0 in Latvia in their opening game, then needed a late Zlatan Ibrahimovic to salvage a 1–1 draw at home to Hungary. In April 2003, the **return of Larsson** to the line-up prompted a 2–1 win over the Hungarians in Budapest, with Marcus Allbäck getting both Swedish goals.

When a national team is struggling for goals, it needs a game against San Marino. Luckily for Sweden, that's exactly what they got. Matthias Jonson hit a rare hat-trick in a 6–0 romp in the tiny republic, setting the team up for a home game against Poland four days later which, though Larsson was by now absent again, they won comfortably, 3–0.

A further meaningless 5–0 win over San Marino followed, but the key game was the return in Poland on 10 September. After Latvia had beaten Hungary earlier in the day, Söderberg and Lagerbäck calculated that **their team would be uncatchable** at the top of the table if they could win. In front of a packed crowd in Chorzów, Mikael Nilsson scored early from a set piece, then Mellberg added a second eight minutes before half-time, again from a set play. When home skipper Tomasz Hajto was sent-off on the hour for apparently elbowing Allbäck, Polish heads began to drop and the Swedes knew they were through.

How they'll play

Given the importance they attach to team spirit, Söderberg and Lagerbäck are known to favour selecting a settled side whenever they can. If the framework is solid, they argue, the side **can survive a drop-out** – even it is a major one. Sweden's experience in qualifying certainly proved the point. When the previously ultra-reliable goalkeeper Magnus Hedman went through a rough patch, 21-year-old Andreas Isaakson was drafted in and immediately made the place his own. Similarly, while the Swedes would still ideally have Henrik Larsson leading their line, his absence for most of the last couple of years has allowed another youngster, Zlatan Ibrahimovic, to mature quickly. The more experienced Allbäck can act as a useful foil upfront, as could Matias Jonsson or Niklas Skoog.

In midfield, where many Swedish sides have historically done their best work, the current squad relies heavily on the English-based pair of Fredrik Ljüngberg and Anders Svensson. Ljüngberg, especially, has been **a dependable provider** of scoring chances for Sweden ever since the Euro 2000 qualifiers, though some critics in the country feel he could score more himself.

Mikael Nilsson and Andreas Jakobsson are the nominal holding players, though other choices abound, among them Johan Mjällby – once a regular starter for Sweden before suffering a series of niggling injuries – and Kim Källström, who is considered one of his country's **brightest hopes** for the future.

At the back, Sweden's dearest wish must be that their steady line of four – Erik Edman, Michael Svensson, Ollof Mellberg and Teddy Lucic – can all stay free of injury. If not, the accomplished cover looks thin on the ground, although Mjällby has successfully played in deeper positions for both club and country, and Petter Hansson, though barely capped by his country so far, has become a more flexible player since moving to Holland.

Who calls the shots

"Lars is the tactical genius; I'm the players' man," is how Tommy Söderberg once described his strange but somehow **successful relationship** with Lars Lagerbäck in the Swedish dugout. Söderberg has been in charge of the national side since 1997, and initially inherited Lagerbäck as his assistant from his predecessor, Tommy Svensson. Two years later Söderberg 'promoted' Lagerbäck, giving him equal status in the minds of both the players and the Swedish game's administrators.

It was a weird idea, but it worked. Sweden qualified in style for Euro 2000 – the partnership's first serious test – and it could be argued that only injuries and other fitness worries have prevented the partnership from being more successful than it has been.

At the start of this year, Söderberg announced he would be **quitting his job** at the end of the finals in Portugal, leaving Lagerbäck in sole charge. Before then, the duo have one last chance to equal Svensson's record and guide the Swedes into the last four of a major tournament. The cynics would argue that the same fitness problems which have bedevilled Sweden in the last two tournaments will plague them again in Portugal. To which Söderberg and Lagerbäck might usefully reply that having Rivaldo and Ronaldo warming benches for their clubs in the run-up to the last World Cup did not do Brazil any harm in 2002.

Group D: Czech Republic

For the third European Championship in a row, the Czechs find themselves drawn in a 'group of death'. For the third time in a row, they are not among the favourites to survive it. And, since they are traditionally one of Europe's more enigmatic teams, it is anyone's guess whether they will prove the doubters wrong, as they did at Euro '96, or whether they will go home early despite playing some nice football, as happened at Euro 2000.

Failure to qualify for either of the World Cups in between these European tournaments has resulted in a series of changes among the back-room staff, but on the field of play the country's line-up has been very consistent, the first-team composition evolving slowly rather than being turned upside-down by each new coach. At a time when many international players from the same country barely seem to know each other, this continuity has worked well for the Czechs, whose elegant, one-touch football demands a strong sense of cohesion.

Not that the squad lacks individual stars. Pavel Nedved is the current European Footballer of the Year, having been the pivotal figure in Juventus' 2002/03 Champions League campaign. On the opposite side of midfield, Tomáš Rosický is a younger, less polished but equally majestic talent. And in attack, the Czechs have the towering Jan Koller to give them an aerial outlet if their considered passing movements aren't cutting it.

In Group D, where so much will be at stake in every game, the Czech Republic's task will be formidable. Happily for them, so is the team.

Who they are

Before 1992 and the so-called 'Velvet Divorce' which separated the Czech and Slovak Republics into two independent states, the top footballers from the two nations played together as Czechoslovakia. The team reached the World Cup final as early as 1934, losing 2–1 to Italy after extra time, and after World War II Czechoslovakia repeated the feat by reaching the 1962 final, where they were beaten 3–1 by Brazil. In both games the Czechs had taken the lead only to be pegged back by **comical goalkeeping errors**.

At the 1976 European Nations Cup finals, it looked as though history would repeat itself. Czechoslovakia were 2–1 up against West Germany in Belgrade when their poor marking allowed the Germans to equalise in the last minute. The game went into extra time and then to a penalty shoot-out, memorably settled by Czechoslovakia's Antonín Panenka, who audaciously chipped the ball into the net while Germany's 'keeper Sepp Maier dived in vain to his right. Beating the then world champions to win such a prize was the high point in Czechoslovakia's football history. The problem for the Czechs is that many key members of the Class of '76 **were actually Slovaks** and, though many pundits cite the victory as evidence of the Czechs' ability at European level, many Czech fans and players do not.

Instead, they point to Euro '96 and the team that lost its own final to Germany – at Wembley after Patrik Berger had given the Czechs the lead from the penalty spot – as the high point in their history so far. For the Czechs, this is **living history**, for Berger and a number of his squad colleagues from that tournament are still very much in contention for a place at Euro 2004.

It's an indication of how much faith the Czechs have in their star players that so many of them have remained part of the national setup for so long. In many other countries, a team that failed to get through the first round of a tournament like Euro 2000 would be **dismantled and reassembled**. But current coach Karel Brückner, who was assistant to Jozef Chovanec in the Low Countries, knows that the side deserved better than the narrow defeats by Holland and France which consigned them to their fate.

Pavel Nedved, Czech and European Player of the Year for 2003

Rather than chop and change, Brückner has **refined the formula** which so nearly worked in 2000, making the odd change in personnel here and there but leaving the team's style and attitude intact. His hope is that, after an excellent qualifying campaign, fresh confidence will allow the Czechs to escape 'death' this time around.

How they got here

Before the qualifying round began, the bookies made the Dutch favourites to finish top of Group 3, with the Czech Republic level with Austria in the betting for second spot and a place in the play-offs. The group also contained two improving former Soviet republics, Belarus and Moldova, with no obvious candidate for the wooden spoon in the shape of a San Marino or a Liechtenstein.

With the Austrians losing 3–0 at home to Holland and then 1–0 away to Moldova, and Belarus being easier meat than had been expected, the group quickly became **a two-horse race** between the Czechs and the Dutch. At the first meeting between the two, in Rotterdam on 29 March 2003, Ruud van Nistelrooy gave Holland the lead with a header from Edgar Davids' cross in stoppage time at the end of the first half. On 68 minutes, Brückner replaced a clearly half-fit Rosický with Milan Baroš, and with virtually his first touch, the young Liverpool striker rolled the ball into the path of Koller for the big man to prod it home for the equaliser.

By the time of the return in Prague the following September, it was a case of 'winner takes all' with top spot at stake and automatic place in Portugal at stake. Roared on by their home crowd, the Czechs began at a **terrific pace**, and Holland's Davids was booked after ten minutes for a clumsy challenge on Nedved. Four minutes later, Karel Poborský was felled by Davids in the box; the Dutchman was sent off and Koller despatched the penalty. Twenty minutes later, Nedved played the rampant Poborsky into space and the former Manchester United man lobbed the ball over Erwin van der Saar and into the net.

The Netherlands pulled one back on the hour through Rafael van der Vaar's deflected shot, but as the Dutch poured forward in search of an equaliser they left gaps at the back, and Baroš punished them with the **last kick of the game**. Final score 3–1, leaving the fans in ecstasy, the Czechs in Portugal and Holland in the play-offs.

How they'll play

The Czech Republic's run of 19 games unbeaten under Brückner has not been achieved without stability. Ten players started at least seven out of the Czechs' eight qualifying matches, and although there is cover for most positions, the coach would prefer not to have to use it.

The team is at its youngest at the back, where Petr Cech – recently signed by Chelsea – established himself as the nation's number one before the play-offs, Brückner having promoted him from the Czech Republic's European Under-21 Championship-winning side of 2002. In front of him, another member of that young side, Zdenek Grygera, takes his place alongside Tomáš Ujfaluši, Martin Jiránek and René Bolf. Yet another promising youngster, Tomáš Hübschman, is available as a more attack-minded option if the going gets tough.

Historically the Czechs have tended to **pack their midfield** and the current side is no exception, with Tomáš Galásek and Marek Jankulovski likely to anchor things, while Rosický and Poborský offer width and Nedved pulls the strings from the centre of the park. The presence on the bench of Patrik Berger, Vladimír Šmicer and Roman Týce, with nearly 200 caps between them and years of experience in some of Europe's top leagues, gives an indication of the strength in-depth the Czechs have in this department.

Upfront, the giant Koller continues to impress, not just with his sheer physical presence but with his first touch and ability to bring runners into play – rare attributes for a player of his height. Brückner's **favoured forward combination** is to deploy Koller as a lone striker with a second front-runner – ideally the excellent but injury-prone Baroš, with Vratislav Lokvenc and Jiří Štajner available as deputies – picking up the pieces.

Who calls the shots

Appearances can be deceptive. With his shock of slicked-back white hair and gruff demeanour, Karel Brückner can look like an extra from a movie about Mozart than a top-level football coach. Yet, much like England's Bobby Robson, Brückner is an **elder statesman** in the Czech game who, despite his long years of experience, still keeps in touch with – and is respected by – the youngest generations of players.

The foundation for this mutual respect is Brückner's involvement with the Czech Republic's youth teams. He coached the Under-23 side at the Sydney Olympics in 2000 and then guided the Under-21s to runners-up spot in the European Championship. Two years later the Czechs would go one better and take the European crown, and although, by that time, Brückner had been given the top job, the Under-21s provided him with plenty of ideas for how the first team could be enriched and improved.

Unlike so many of the coaches at Euro 2004, Brückner enjoyed only modest success at club level before he began work in the international setup. His first job was with the Slovak club Inter Bratislava, while subsequent appointments took him back to the Czech Republic with Sigma Olomouc and FK Drnovice – hardly the **stuff of legend**.

Germany

Having gone from the ridiculous to the sublime during his first two years in charge of Germany, coach Rudi Völler is cautiously optimistic about his team's chances in Portugal. You might think that a man who had led his side to a World Cup final against Brazil two years ago would be urging his men to on to greater glory. But Völler argues that the European Championship is a tougher test, and that it is Germany's disastrous display at Euro 2000 – when they failed to win a match and finished bottom of their first-round group – that should be the yardstick for Euro 2004.

You might argue that this is no more than clever spin-doctoring on Völler's part. Using his favoured comparison, he could argue that a quarter-final exit in Portugal is a step in the right direction, even though Germany's

Germany sometimes made hard work of their qualifiers – Christian Wörns tries
to get the better of Iceland's Eidur Gudjohnsen

footballing public would see it as a failure. But he does have a point. There's
no doubt that the 'group of death' in which the Germans find themselves
this summer is infinitely tougher than their opening section in Japan/Korea
two years ago. And the going will only get tougher as the tournament
wears on.

When he says is he is quietly confident, of course Völler is deliberately
lowering public expectations. He's doing it partly out of respect for the
quality of Germany's opponents in Group D, and partly, perhaps, because of
his own realisation that reaching the World Cup final two years ago might
not have been quite the towering achievement his country's own media
made it out to be at the time.

Who they are

Statisticians continue to argue over how many historical **football accolades** to grant
the Germans. The nation achieved little before World War II, and the post-war

division of the country into East and West meant that, until 1990, there were always two Germanies competing for honours. The communist-run east of the country had never been much of a football stronghold, even in pre-war days. Aside from the 1974 World Cup, when the team from the East beat that of the West 1–0 in a group game, 'East Germany' rarely featured as an international force.

'West Germany', on the other hand, got the post-war era **off to a flyer** when, very much the underdogs in the 1954 final, they won the World Cup by beating Hungary 3–2 in Berne. Eight years later, with Helmut Schön as coach, Uwe Seeler leading the line and a young defender called Franz Beckenbauer, the West Germans made it to the final again, only to lose 4–2 to their hosts, England.

In 1970 Beckenbauer played through the pain barrier with his **arm in a sling** against Italy in the World Cup semi-final, but his team lost 4–3. Two years later, though, and Schön's side would begin to garner the silverware their football deserved. With Beckenbauer inventing his own 'libero' role for himself and the goal-hungry Gerd Müller upfront, West Germany beat the Soviet Union 3–0 to lift the European Nations Cup in Brussels, then added the World Cup on home soil, coming from behind to beat Holland 2–1 in the final in Munich.

Defeat by Czechoslovakia in the Nations Cup final of 1976 heralded the end of Beckenbauer's 'total football' era, and when the West Germans next won the competition, by beating Belgium 2–1 in the final in Rome, it was with a rather workmanlike team in which deep-lying forward Karl-Heinz Rummenigge was the only great creative force.

Beckenbauer returned to the fold to coach West Germany to victory in the 1990 World Cup, with a team built around midfield powerhouse Lothar Matthäus and spectacular striker Jürgen Klinsmann. Beckenbauer's assistant Berti Vogts then took over for Euro '92, integrating players from **the former East Germany** into a unified German team for the first time. The side began as favourites but were surprisingly beaten in the final, 2–0 by Denmark. Four years later it was a different story, as Vogts' team, now inspired by former East German international Matthias Sammer, beat the Czech Republic 2–1 to be crowned kings of Europe for a record third time.

Vogts' resignation after the 1998 World Cup left a **power vacuum** within the national side, and it was the hapless Erich Ribbeck who guided Germany through their win-less Euro 2000 campaign, his decision to recall a 39-year-old Matthäus coming back to haunt him as Germany's captain trudged disconsolately off the pitch at the end of the final 3–0 humiliation by Portugal.

How they got here

The Germans were clear favourites to win a qualifying section also containing Scotland, Iceland, Lithuania and the Faroe Isles, but although they finished on top, the road wasn't as smooth as it was supposed to be.

A brilliant long-range effort by Michael Ballack set up a 2–0 win in Lithuania in Germany's opening game, and after the same player put them ahead after only two minutes at home to the Faroes in Hannover, a big score looked on the cards. In the end, only Miroslav Klose's second-half header separated the teams, after Arne Friedrich's own-goal had allowed the Faroese to draw level on the stroke of half-time. Worse was to come in March 2003, when Lithuania came away from Nuremberg with a 1–1 draw – again after the Germans had taken an early lead.

Völler called that game "a wake-up call" but his players didn't heed it. Germany **continued to drop points**, being held 1–1 by Berti Vogts' Scotland in Glasgow in June, then 0–0 in Iceland. With both of those countries still in with a chance of winning the group, the Germans needed to win their home games against them to be sure of top spot.

Against Scotland in Dortmund, a controversial penalty by Ballack gave the Germans a rare two-goal cushion and allowed them to run out 2–1 winners against spirited opponents, while in Hamburg a month later, an early Ballack goal **settled the nerves** and set Germany on the way to a 3–0 win – the first time Völler's side had scored more than twice in the entire campaign.

How they'll play

Völler has plenty of options at this disposal but, as at the World Cup two years ago, it's a case of 'spot the flair player'. Whichever formation Völler opts for, he knows that most of his team's goal opportunities are going to come through Ballack, either as provider or as goalscorer himself.

It's not that the Germans lack strikers. Fredi Bobic came back into form for his country during the qualifying campaign, while Stuttgart's youngster Kevin Kuranyi has had an impressive year and Miroslav Klose is normally a **calm finisher**. It's the ability to bring others into an attack that sets Ballack apart, and if there is nobody else around, there's always the Bayern Munich playmaker's long-range shooting to fall back on.

In the circumstances, it's just as well that the Germans have width, with Oliver Neuville, Torsten Frings, Jörg Böhme and, if he can recover from his mental-health problems in time, Sebastian Deisler all capable of worrying opposing full-backs, and of providing the kind of crosses Germany's **penalty-box predators** will thrive on.

The remainder of Völler's midfield is likely to comprise 'holding' players, with the fit-again Didi Hamann capable of playing a key role, and Jens Jeremies, Bernd Schneider and Carsten Ramelow also in contention for a place.

At the back, the coach faces something of a dilemma, albeit a nice one to have. Christian Wörns is the obvious **stopper-in-chief** if Völler opts for 4–4–2, but the revival in form of Jens Nowotny, a more creative *libero* in the Beckenbauer or Sammer mould, gives Germany the option of playing 3–5–2 – something the team may well try in Portugal against the inventive Czechs and Dutch.

As well as dependable defensive anchors, the Germans also boast a number of youngsters who could add some much-needed pace to the backline, among them Arne Friedrich, Sebastian Kehl, Tobias Rau and Philipp Lahm.

Youth is not on the side of Germany's regular goalkeepers, but who cares that your number one will be 35 years old on the eve of the tournament when his name is Oliver Kahn?

Who calls the shots

Rudi Völler never intended to be a coach. After a playing career that had taken him to Werder Bremen, AS Roma and Olympique Marseille among other clubs, he hung up his boots at Bayer Leverkusen and got **an administrator's job** there.

Then, when Erich Ribbeck resigned in the wake of Germany's poor showing at Euro 2000, Völler stepped in as caretaker coach of the national team while his friend Christoph Daum, who was due to take over in 2001, served out his contract at Leverkusen. Events then overtook both men. Daum was embroiled in a **drugs scandal** and was forced to resign, and although Völler initially wanted to return to Leverkusen to take his place, the German FA, the DFB, persuaded him to stay on as national-team boss.

In his first season Völler survived England's 5–1 thumping of Germany in Munich and managed to guide his side all the way through the play-offs to the final of the 2002 World Cup itself. There they tried – and only narrowly failed – to emulate the achievements of their mentor, who has a World Cup winner's medal from 1990 in his **trophy cabinet** at home.

Holland

Did Scotland do the Dutch a huge favour by beating them 1–0 in the first leg of their Euro 2004 play-off? That's the question many among the sports media in Holland, not to mention ordinary fans, have begun to ask themselves as the big kick-off approaches.

Prior to the game in Glasgow and the 3–1 defeat by the Czech Republic in Prague which forced the Netherlands into the play-off in the first place, all had seemed relatively well in the House of Orange. Coach Dick Advocaat had brought confidence back to a side which had failed to qualify for the last World Cup, and though the team had a very familiar look to it – based as it was on a backbone of players from Ajax's 1995 Champions League triumph – nobody cared so long as they were good to watch and the results kept coming.

The defeat by the Czechs came as a huge shock to the system, but the pain wasn't really felt until James McFadden's goal gave the Scots a shock win at Hampden and put Holland's place at Euro 2004 in real jeopardy. After the match, Advocaat publicly accused some of his players of ignoring his instructions and "going backwards". And while he refused to name names, the coach's team-sheet for the return leg in Amsterdam told its own story: defender Frank de Boer and striker Patrick Kluivert, two men who typified the Ajax 'old guard', had been dropped.

Airing their laundry – public disputes are nothing new to the Dutch, as Kluivert and Davids showed during qualifying

The results were sensational. Holland brushed the Scots aside 6–0, playing with such a degree of confidence and panache, it was hard to imagine any of the same players had taken part in the first leg four days earlier.

The fear now for the Dutch is that although Advocaat appears, albeit by accident, to have found a formula that works for Euro 2004, there is not much time left to refine it. Many of the players who shone in Amsterdam are young, and the opposition in Portugal will be rather trickier than Berti Vogts' bravehearts.

Who they are

Considering the esteem in which Dutch football is rightly held today, it is hard to imagine that before 1974, Holland had never appeared in the finals of a major tournament. Yet for much of the post-war period, football in the Netherlands was an amateur pursuit, played almost **for the hell of it** by small clubs part-owned by local town councils.

All that changed at the end of the 1960s when coach Rinus Michels and an immensely gifted young forward by the name of Johan Cruyff fashioned a new kind of Dutch team at Ajax of Amsterdam. Ajax dominated not just the Dutch league but the European scene as well, and when Cruyff brought Holland's national side to the

1974 World Cup finals, their unique brand of **'total football'**, in which players swapped roles constantly during the course of a game, took the world by storm. The Dutch brushed the likes of Italy and Brazil aside on their way to the final but were beaten 2–1 by the hosts West Germany.

Four years later, with Cruyff now absent but many of the Class of '74 still in the team, the Dutch again made it to the World Cup final and, again, were unlucky to lose to the host nation – on this occasion Argentina.

Holland then faded from view until a new-generation team, built around the AC Milan trio of Frank Rijkaard, Ruud Gullit and Marco van Basten, arrived in Germany for the European Championship of 1988. In contrast to earlier Dutch sides, this one began nervously but **gradually found its form**, van Basten scoring a hat-trick to eliminate England, a late winner to knock the Germans out in the semi-finals, and a spectacular second to wrap up victory against the Soviet Union in the final.

The Germans would get their revenge over Holland in the second round of the World Cup two years later, and the Dutch did not really blossom again until 1998, when a third generation of stars – spearheaded once again by former Ajax stars such as Dennis Bergkamp, Marc Overmars, the de Boer brothers and Edgar Davids – came within an inch of knocking Brazil out of the World Cup, then lost on penalties to Italy in the semi-finals of Euro 2000, a tournament the Dutch had co-hosted with the Belgians and been expected to win.

How they got here

Out-thought by the Czechs in Prague, out-fought by the Scots in Glasgow, Dick Advocaat's side finally showed their fans what they could do when a revised line-up took the field in the play-off second leg against Scotland in Amsterdam on 19 June.

Midfielder Wesley Sneijder **opened the floodgates** after just 13 minutes when he turned Barry Ferguson and rifled an unstoppable shot past Rab Douglas to level the scores on aggregate. The same player then set up two more goals from set pieces on Scotland's left flank, the first for André Ooijer, the second for Ruud van Nistelrooy. They were the sort of balls into the box that the Scots had dealt with comfortably five days earlier, but now, with the heat turned up, the visitors' composure melted.

After half-time, van Nistelrooy chipped the ball over Douglas to make it 4–0, Frank de Boer came on as a substitute and struck the fifth from a corner, and finally van Nistelrooy completed his hat-trick, turning in a cross by Andy van der Meyde.

In truth, it was not quite the **classic display** of 'total football' that some commentators described it as. But it was more like the real Holland – cool, confident, ever-ready to turn on the style.

How they'll play

Nobody debates tactics in public like the Dutch. Over the years, star after star – from Cruyff to Gullit to Kluivert – has fallen out with coaching staff over the right approach to take, and either walked out or managed to get the coach sacked. Dick

Advocaat seems in little danger of getting the shove himself, but it might have been a close call had Holland failed to qualify for Euro 2004.

As it is, Advocaat has accepted that he's been guilty of sticking with established players for too long in the past, and that he has to be careful not to make the same mistake again. This is **music to the ears** of Holland's younger players, some of whom have perhaps been waiting too long to get their chance at full international level.

Like his German counterpart Rudi Völler, Advocaat has the flexibility to play with a sweeper or with a flat back-four. This makes the precise formation of players in front of first-choice 'keeper Edwin van der Sar hard to forecast, particularly as the coach himself has said he will **keep shuffling his pack** for as long as he has to name his squad for the finals.

However, Jaap Stam seems certain to be somewhere at the heart of defence, as does Frank de Boer despite being relegated to the subs bench for the play-off second leg against the Scots. André Ooijer stands a good chance of ousting Giovanni van Bronckhorst from the right-back role, while Michael Reiziger and Philip Cocu are two left-sided options.

In midfield, the combination of Sneijder and Rafael van der Vaart worked brilliantly against the Scots in Amsterdam, but Advocaat will want to look at other options – not least because van der Vaart, especially, is a versatile player who can adopt a number of attacking roles. It will be hard to ignore the claims of Edgar Davids for a holding role, while there is a whole **glut of wide players** for the Dutch to choose from, including Andy van der Meyde, Clarence Seedorf and Boudewijn Zenden, not to mention those who can also play wing-back in a 3–5–2 formation such as Reiziger and Cocu.

In attack, the obvious **focus of attention** will be van Nistelrooy, who missed Euro 2000 through injury and has been desperate for a big international stage to play on ever since. The Manchester United star's inability to forge a working partnership with Patrick Kluivert may force Advocaat to decide on one or the other, with the more self-effacing Roy Makaay one candidate to play alongside van Nistelrooy if, as many in Holland now expect, Kluivert is relegated to the bench.

Who calls the shots

Not many national-team bosses get a second bite at the cherry, and having taken Holland to the quarter-finals of the World Cup first time around, Dick Advocaat is determined to go further this time.

Advocaat's **return to the top job** was not scheduled. But nobody anticipated that former Ajax captain Frank Rijkaard would resign after Holland's semi-final defeat by Italy at Euro 2000, or that Rijkaard's mentor Louis van Gaal, who succeeded him as coach of *de Oranje*, would fail to get the team to the 2002 World Cup at all.

After his second call-up, Advocaat initially tried juggling being coach of the Netherlands with an administrative role at Rangers, the Glasgow club he coached between 1998 and 2001. But in November 2002 he decided the Dutch job was too big and left Ibrox altogether.

Latvia

On 25 April 2001, no more than 500 souls gathered in Riga to see Marians Pahars open the scoring for Latvia against San Marino with less than a minute played of a World Cup qualifier. Just before the hour mark, Nicola Albani equalised for the visitors. There was no further scoring.

It was the worst result in Latvia's brief footballing history and, in a sense, also one of the best. For the humiliation of failing to beat probably the weakest national team in Europe, and on home soil to boot, was too much for their English-born coach, Gary Johnson, to take. He stepped down after the game, paving the way for his assistant, Aleksandrs Starkovs, to take charge. Just two and a half years later, Starkovs and his players would be celebrating qualification for Euro 2004 in Istanbul, the team having beaten World Cup bronze medallists Turkey 3–2 in the play-offs to book their place in the finals.

It's not so much that the transformation in Latvia's fortunes can be put down solely to a change of coach. On the contrary, during his two years in the job, Johnson succeeded in changing the mentality of the Latvian side

Fantasy football – Imants Bleidelis (left) and Mihails Zemlinskis hug Alex Kolinko after his last-minute penalty save in Sweden

which, until that point, had concentrated on trying to avoid defeat, rather than trying to win games. At the same time, the accession of the locally born Starkovs, who enjoys near legendary status in the Latvian game, to the position of head coach gave the players a renewed sense of focus and provided a much-needed boost for their fragile confidence.

In the build-up to Euro 2004, confidence remains Starkovs' watchword. He has refused to arrange friendlies against top-class opposition, even though his team have been drawn in the 'group of death' in Portugal. He believes it will be better for Latvia to keep their winning habit rather than suffer potentially morale-shattering defeats. And though some critics might question the logic of this approach, when a man has accomplished the kind of turnaround that Starkovs has effected with Latvia, you tend not to argue.

Who they are

When the Soviet Union began to disintegrate at the start of the 1990s, it was the Baltic states – Lithuania, Latvia and Estonia – that broke away first. Just over a decade later, and all three countries are poised to join the European Union. In a very short space of time, all three have become modern democracies operating a free-market economy. Yet in footballing terms, none was thought to have the potential of some of the bigger former Soviet republics such as the Ukraine, Georgia or Belarus.

Part of the reason for this is the **popularity of other sports** in the Baltics. Basketball is practically a national obsession in Lithuania, while for the Latvians and Estonians, winter sports such as ice-hockey are the dominant force. Latvia, a country of more than two million people, can muster only 12 professional clubs and just over 100 registered players. Its domestic league is one of the least competitive in Europe, with Skonto Riga having won the title in each of the last 11 years.

Yet every cloud has its silver lining. The very fact that Skonto are so dominant has given their players regular outings in the qualifying rounds of the Champions League. This in turn has put many **in the shop window** for transfers overseas, with Pahars already a notable success story at Southampton.

And, like the Slovenes at Euro 2000, Latvia's footballers believe that the publicity generated by their run to the finals will translate into a fresh enthusiasm for football among the local population. Their unlikely victory in Turkey made them heroes overnight, and the air of expectancy – not least after Slovenia's robust showing in the Low Countries four years ago – can only intensify between now and the big kick-off. Europe may feel that it is more than ready for Latvia, but the feeling is mutual.

How they got here

Nobody could accuse the Latvians of taking an easy route to the finals. Drawn in Group 4 alongside Sweden, Poland, Hungary and San Marino (again), according to the FIFA rankings they **should have finished fourth**. But right from the word go, there were signs that Starkovs' counter-attacking style was going to pay off.

In their first game in September 2002, the Latvians held Sweden 0–0 at home, and although much of the game was spent mounting a rearguard action, the underdogs managed to create some chances of their own. The next match was even better – a stunning 1–0 win over Poland in Warsaw, after Juris Laizans' long-range shot had eluded Jerzy Dudek on the half-hour.

Latvia's San Marino jinx looked as though it was going to return to haunt them in November until a **last-minute own goal** brought a 1–0 win away from home, and a 3–0 victory over the same opponents in April 2003 saw Starkovs' side sitting pretty, three points clear at the top of the group table.

Maris Verpakovskis then gave Latvia the lead away to Hungary in June, but the team were second-best on the day and didn't deserve better than the 3–1 defeat the Magyars inflicted on them. Having conceded their first goals of the campaign, Latvia let in two more in the first half at home to Poland, and suddenly top spot was **no more than a memory**.

Weaker teams might have wilted at this point, but Starkovs knew his side were still in with a shout, and a 3–1 win at home to Hungary, inspired by Verpakovskis' fine solo opener, saw Latvia's hopes revived just four days after the loss to the Poles. Sweden's victory in Poland the same day had sealed top spot, but in a sense that worked in Latvia's favour, for the Swedes had little to play for when they entertained Starkovs' side in their final group game in October. After Verpakovskis had given Latvia the lead, they survived the dismissal of Dzintars Zirnis and a last-minute penalty by Marcus Allbäck which goalkeeper Aleksandrs Kolinko tipped over the crossbar.

The win was enough to put Latvia in the play-offs but, when they were paired with Turkey, few gave them a chance. Those critics had reckoned without Verpakovskis, who scored **another great individual goal** to win the first leg in Riga 1–0, and whose breakaway strike 14 minutes from time in Istanbul – after Jurijs Laizans' flukey free-kick had given the team a precious away goal – sealed a 3–2 aggregate scoreline. Latvia's remarkable journey was complete.

How they'll play

If counter-attack was generally the order of the day for Latvia in qualifying, then there's even less likelihood of any variation in the menu come the finals. Coach Starkovs, however, **dislikes the sweeper system** and tends to prefer spreading a flat back-four in front of the spectacular if occasionally error-prone Kolinko.

Mihails Zemlinskis and Igors Stepanovs are the first-choice central defenders, while Zimis and Aleksandrs Isakovs were regulars in the full-back positions during the qualifiers. Crucially for the Starkovs game plan, all have a good turn of speed as well as being solid, reliable man-markers.

In midfield, Latvia's hard work ethic finds eager employees in Valentins Lobanovs and Vitalis Astafjevs, while Imants Bleidelis and Andrejs Rubins offer pace on the flanks, with Rubins in particular enjoying the odd cut inside as well as having the ability to deliver **a telling cross or two**.

Upfront, the long-term injury which afflicted Pahars for most of 2003 appears to have eased, but he may be hard-pressed to win back a first-team place if Verpakovskis continues his **impetuous run of form**. Vits Rimkus, nominally an auxiliary striker, can operate in a deeper role if Latvia are defending a lead and want to press the ball harder in midfield.

Who calls the shots

For obvious reasons, coach Starkovs has come to embody Latvia's transformation from **cowards to contenders**. His own playing career was marked by courage and determination (while playing for Daugava Riga, he became the first Latvian to score 100 goals in the former Soviet Supreme League), and as a club coach he has masterminded Skonto Riga's domination of the domestic game.

Starkovs' three years as assistant to Gary Johnson in the national setup involved a **steep learning curve** for both men, with Johnson trying to change deeply ingrained attitudes among players who were clearly more talented than their tactics permitted them to show, and Starkovs framing an outline of what was and wasn't possible.

Johnson returned to England in 2001 and became **manager of Yeovil Town**, though he remains a consultant to the Latvian FA and is their honorary president. Starkovs, meanwhile, is having to alter his own ideas of what is and isn't possible, with a team that is already living in the realms of fantasy football.

Portugal's
eight venues
explained
and explored

The Cities

Aveiro

The tourist board bill Aveiro as the Venice of Portugal, which is as much a misnomer as its football team. There are a few canals in Aveiro, but Venice it isn't, just as the local team, **Beira-Mar** ('By the Sea') are actually located some way inland. Nevertheless, Aveiro is attractive enough in a low-key way, and it is certainly within reach of some fine sandy beaches.

Aveiro's canals were dug in the 1800s after its harbour silted up, and today's economy still revolves around fishing and salt – you'll see the huge saltpans in the shallow lagoons just outside town, and colourful fishing boats still line the central canal.

Like the town, Beira-Mar rarely make the headlines, though recent years have looked promising for the club. They won the Portuguese cup in 1999, qualifying for Europe for the first time in the process. In season 2003/04 they looked set to better their highest-ever league position of 6th in 1991. They boast former Leeds and Ajax player Clyde Wijnhard and former Welsh international 'keeper Andy Marriot in their ranks.

Getting there

Aveiro lies on the fast **Alfa train line** from Lisbon, Coimbra and Porto, with a service roughly hourly to each city (under one hour to Coimbra and Porto, around 2.5 hours to Lisbon). Both the train and bus stations lie to the northeast of town: head down Avenida Dr Lourenço Peixinho for fifteen minutes and you'll see the Canal Centrale. Aveiro is a short drive from the main **Lisbon–Porto motorway**: allow 2.5 hours' drive from Lisbon, and half an hour to Porto or Coimbra.

Getting around

Aveiro is small enough to walk around, though as it is very flat, cycling is an excellent way to see its sights. **Bikes** are available free from the BUGA kiosk on the main square, Praça Humberto Delgado, by the Canale Central.

The tourist office lies just to the right as you face the canal on Rua João **Mendonça 8** (daily 9am–8pm) and can supply maps and details of local events. They can also give details of boat trips, which depart from in front of the tourist office around the lagoon.

It is also worth checking out bus times to the local beaches. The 9km-run to the nearest of these, at **Barra and Costa Nova**, takes about 30 minutes. To get to the stadium, special bus services will be laid on, with departures from the central Praça Humberto Delgado.

2 July 2000 – Desailly, Deschamps and
Leboeuf hold the trophy aloft

20 June 1976 – Czechoslovakia's Antonin Panenka, having swapped shirts with his West German opposite number, kisses the trophy in Belgrade

France's Michel Platini (far left) wheels away after scoring while Belgian 'keeper Jean-Marie Pfaff appeals in vain for offside, 1984

Portugal's Luís Figo wants more movement
from a free-kick against France, 2000

Holland's Marco van Basten dominates the
final against the Soviet Union, 1988

Pre-match entertainment organised by the Croatian FA for the travelling support
from Slovenia – Zagreb, November 2003

Italy's Alessandro del Piero is inconsolable after his misses cost Italy the
Championship in the 2000 final against France

The Bulgarian defence clear its lines in Andorra with more mountains than people in attendance, September 2003

Germany's Karl-Heinz Riedle feels the force of Danish resistance during the 1992 final, which Denmark won against the odds

Class of '96: Gascoigne, Sheringham,
Anderton and McManaman at Wembley

Lisbon's José Alvalade stadium, one of
eight new arenas to be built for Euro 2004

Latvia's Vitas Rimkus (right) is hit on the back by a bottle thrown from the crowd after his team score their first goal against Turkey in Istanbul, November 03

New European and long haul destinations feature in TAP Air Portugal's summer schedule.

In recognition of the increasing popularity of Madeira in both the leisure and conference/incentive markets in the UK, an additional service has been introduced to Funchal from Gatwick.

SUMMER

This brings the number of direct weekly services between London and Funchal to five. Passengers have risen year on year to Brazil since 1999. Last year TAP Air Portugal carried over 530,000 passengers. To cope with this increasing demand all existing destinations, São Paulo, Rio de Janeiro, Salvador, Fortaleza and Recife, now have daily services from Lisbon.

In addition, for the period June-September a service to Natal has been introduced three times a week. This will bring the number of flights operated from Portugal to Brazil up to 38 per week – more than any other European airline.

Staying over

Much of Aveiro's top-end accommodation was already booked up in 2003, and rooms in this small town are sure to be in short supply. **Residencial Albôi** (☎234 380 390), in a quiet side street on Rua da Arrocheira 6, offers good-value doubles or triples, all with cable TV and breakfast, from €55 a double. Right in the centre, overlooking the canal, **Hotel Arcada** (☎234 423 001) on Rua de Viana do Castelo 4 has small rooms but with ensuite facilities for €75 a double. **Residencial Palmeira** (☎234 422 521) on Rua da Palmeira 7 offers bright rooms with TV and breakfast from €50 in a modern building in the old town. Pensão **Residencial Estrela** (☎234 423 818) on Rua José Estevão 4 is a characterful guest house with plant-filled communal areas and decent doubles from €50, which includes breakfast. Simple but clean with ensuite showers, **A Brasileira** (☎234 428 634) on Rua Tenente Resende is in a good position near the fish market; doubles from €40.

'A giant frisbee with spikes' – Aveiro's distinctive stadium takes shape

Eating, drinking and clubbing

Not surprisingly, fish and shellfish are the specialities of Aveiro. **A Barca**, on Rua José Rabumba 5, is famed for its quality fish at reasonable prices. Other restaurants and bars cluster round the fish market and the canal-side Cais do Batirões. **O Telheiro** on Largo da Praça do Peixe 20–21 has excellent grilled fish for bargain prices, but closes on Saturdays. Nearby **Doca Restaurante**, on Cais do Batirões 24, offers *peixe na telha* (fish cooked on a tile) and other imaginative dishes in a modernised town house facing a canal, with live music most weekends (closed Sundays). For later action, the adjacent **Utopia Bar** at Cais do Batirões 33 (open Tues–Sat) or the more local **Taberna do Cais** at #29 are usually hopping until the small hours.

Venue verdict

For a side used to attendances of 5,000 or under, getting a brand-new purpose-built stadium seating 31,200 is a dream come true for Beira-Mar. The **Estádio Municipal Mario Duarte** was designed by Tomás Tavira, one of Portugal's most famous architects – its sleek lines and rippled roof make it resemble a giant multi-coloured frisbee with spikes.

The stadium lies 5km east of the centre just off the main IP5 towards Lisbon and Porto, in a sports park that includes a golf course, tennis courts, a spa and riding centre. Fixtures for Euro 2004 are **Czech Republic v Latvia** on 15 June, and **Netherlands v Czech Republic** on 19 June.

Braga

Braga means 'knickers' in Spanish, but snigger not: to the Portuguese the town represents the **centre of the catholic church**. The Portuguese for 'as old as the hills' is 'as old as the Cathedral of Braga' and the cathedral here dates from just after the liberation of the town from the Moors in 1070. Though central Braga is grand and ancient – the seventeenth-century **Palácio dos Biscaínhos** ranks as one of the loveliest in the country – today's quiet, pedestrianised old town streets are circled by suburbs of neat modern ring roads and tower blocks, a successful blend of new and old that makes this one of the more appealing of northern Portuguese towns.

Braga's football team are the **Arsenal of Portugal**, but only in so far as they share the same strip. They are one of the more accomplished first division sides and were runners-up in the Portuguese cup in 1998, but the extent of their success is to qualify for Europe, which they have managed in recent seasons through their league position, well behind the leading clubs.

Getting there

It is easiest to get to Braga by **train** – most services go via Porto. The hour's train ride from Porto (departures roughly hourly) pulls in at the station some 15 minutes' walk southwest of the centre. Turn right down Rua Andrade Corvo and keep going under the arch into the old town, until you reach the broad Praça da República, the attractive main square full of spouting fountains

The main **bus station** is a ten-minute walk north of the centre: turn right down Avenida General Norto de Matas and keep going until you see Praça da República. **Motorists** should follow signs from the somewhat confusing ring road to the centre and head to an authorised car park.

Getting around

The centre of Braga is easy to **explore on foot** – indeed most of the narrow streets and wide squares in the old town around Praça da República and the Sé (the cathedral) are pedestrianised, and unusually for a Portuguese town, most of Braga is flat. You're unlikely to need public transport – the town is one of the few venues for Euro 2004 where the stadium is **walkable from the centre** – though buses and taxis are inexpensive.

The **tourist office** (Mon–Fri 9am–7pm, Sat 9am–12.30pm & 2–5.30pm, ☎253 262 550) is on the southern corner of Praça da República and can help out with accommodation and maps of the town.

Staying over

Braga has a shortage of quality accommodation at the best of times, and will be stretched to the limit during Euro 2004. A good place to try is **Hotel Residencial Bragashopping** (☎253 275 722), in a shopping centre on Avenida Central, right on the main square. Despite its unusual position, the hotel's air-conditioned rooms are spacious and can accommodate 1, 2, 3 or 4 people; car parking can also be arranged. Doubles from €40.

Somewhat sterile but good value is **Hotel Ibis** (☎253 610 860) on Rua do Carmo 13, to one side of Braga's other main square, Praça Conde de Agrolongo. Rooms are air-conditioned with satellite TV, and upper ones have good views over town. Doubles cost from €55.

Other central options include **Grande Residencial Avenida** (☎253 609 028), Avenida da Liberdade 738, a slightly fading guesthouse with big rooms on the main avenue from €30 a double; or the more spruce **Residencial dos Terceiros** (☎253 270 466) on Rua dos Capelistas 85, with ensuite bathrooms and TVs in all rooms, from €40 a double.

Eating, drinking and clubbing

Braga has a vibrant café society, with most of the population watching the world go by at some stage or other from **Café Astória** or **Café Vianna**. Both these have chairs and tables spilling out onto the Praça da República and are great places to enjoy beer, coffee or a sandwich. Even more atmospheric is the old-fashioned **A Brasileira** on Largo Barão de São Marinha, with seats outside on the pedestrianised drag.

For late-night action, there are some good bars around Praça Conde de Agrolongo. **Barnova**, in a glass kiosk right in the centre of the square, attracts a young crowd until the small hours, while **Populum Bar** at #115 pumps out the latest dance sounds from Thursday to Saturday until around 5am.

For a full meal, there are plenty of restaurants around the old town. **A Moçambicana**, on Rua Andrade Corvo just outside the town gates on the way to the station offers inexpensive Portuguese cuisine, including some Mozambiquan

Being built into the Monte Castro hillside should work wonders for Braga's stadium acoustics

specialities. More upmarket, **De Bouro** on Rua Santo António das Travessas 30–32, near the cathedral, is a former Cistercian monastic lodge serving meaty specialities from the Minho region (closed Sundays).

Further entertainment can be had at **Bracalânia**, a theme park with fairground rides, including a ferris wheel and helter-skelter, 1km south of town on the way to Bom Jesus. The park stays open until midnight.

Venue verdict

Braga's **Estádio Municipal** is one of the most innovative and exciting of the competition, built from scratch to the designs of eminent architect Eduardo Souto Moura. The structure merges into the Monte Castro hillside, with parts of the hill's base-rock forming a natural amphitheatre. The stadium is also covered, giving welcome shade during the blistering heat of summer. The roof, along with the rock walls, should contribute to some powerful acoustics, though a capacity of just 30,000 makes this one of the smaller Euro 2004 venues.

The stadium lies twenty minutes walk north of the centre – from Praça da República, head down Rua dos Chãos and turn right into Rua Gabriel Perreira, then left into Avenida Artur Soares. Fixtures for the first round are **Bulgaria v Denmark** on 18 June and **Netherlands v Latvia** on 23 June.

Coimbra

Once the capital of Portugal, Coimbra (pronounced 'Queem-bra') is
Portugal's answer to Oxford – an attractive and historic **university town**
set on a river, and full to the brim with the country's academic elite. The
local football team, the appropriately named **Académica**, are currently
mixing it with the big, brainy boys but generally hover among the dullards
of *II Divisão*.

Perhaps not surprisingly, football rarely stirs much passion in a city whose
population deflates outside term-time, and future usage of Coimbra's new
stadium will be shared between football, athletics and other events. A bunch
of rowdy English visitors were certainly made welcome for the stadium's
inauguration, when the Rolling Stones played to a full house, but it remains
to be seen how this friendly, laid-back town reacts to the England football
supporters who will visit for the game with Switzerland on 17 June.

Getting there

Though it feels little more than an average-sized town, Coimbra is nevertheless
Portugal's third city – positioned halfway between Lisbon and Porto. Fast **Alfa trains**
depart roughly hourly from Lisbon's Santa Apolónia station to Coimbra B station,
with the 2.25-hour run costing just €14. Regular local trains link this station with
the central Coimbra A station in the heart of the city – there's no need to get
another ticket.

Motorists should avoid the dense network of **narrow central streets**, head for one
of the out-of-town car parks and walk into the centre. Allow two hours' drive time
from Lisbon, an hour from Porto and a good four hours from Faro.

Getting around

The main **bus station** is around 15 minutes' walk northwest of the city centre; taxis
are inexpensive, or head down Avenida Fernão de Megalhães until you see the train
station, which is right on the edge of the centre by the river Mondego. Opposite
the bridge, Largo da Portagem and the pedestrianised Rua Ferreira Borges represent
the main hub of daytime Coimbra.

The rest of the centre is small enough to get around on foot. Most of the sites of
interest are set on a hill, so you'll need **legs of steel** to negotiate some of its slopes,
especially to the historic university buildings, which include the famous Baroque
Biblioteca Joanina library. Also on the hillside are the Sé Velha (cathedral) and
Museu Machado de Castro, a museum whose Roman crypts are one of Portugal's
more eerie sights.

The **tourist office** (Mon–Fri 9am–7pm, Sat & Sun 10am–1pm & 2.30–5.30pm, ☎239 488 120), just east of the bridge facing the river on Largo da Portagem, gives out maps of the city and can tell you about local events.

Staying over

Hotel accommodation is sure to be in short supply during Euro 2004, but if you are not too fussy about where you stay, there are scores of cheap *pensões* in the network of narrow streets between Coimbra A station and the centre. **Flôr de Coimbra** on Rua do Poço 5 (☎239 823 865) is clean and characterful with rooms of varying size, including plenty of single rooms and some that sleep three. Doubles with shared bathroom cost €35, or €45 for private facilities, and price includes breakfast at its decent restaurant.

Slightly more upmarket, **Residencial Avenida** on the riverfront Avenida Emídio Navarro 37 (☎239 822 156) offers somewhat faded grandeur, including a bar, TV lounge and restaurant, for €50 per double. If your budget can stretch to it, the **Hotel**

Referees with faulty watches won't have far to look to see how much time to add on from the pitch in Coimbra

Astória, Avenida Emídio Navarro 21 (☎239 853 020) offers formal service and Art Nouveau decor for €100 a double.

If you're struggling in Coimbra itself, it may be easier to find accommodation in **Figueira da Foz**, the nearest coastal resort – an hour or so west by bus or train. A hugely popular beach and surfing destination, the town is well geared to hoardes of visitors and there are plenty of inexpensive guesthouses, or take one of the private rooms that are usually touted at the bus and train stations.

Eating, drinking and clubbing

Coimbra's nightlife usually tones down in summertime when the students have left, but no doubt bar and club owners will be keen to cash in on its extra Euro 2004 visitors. There are plenty of cafés and bars around the old centre. Coimbra's most famous café is **Café Santa Cruz** on Praça 8 de Maio, with a vaulted stone interior that used to be a part of a monastery. **Bar Quebra Costas**, on Rua Quebra Costas 47 on the way up to the cathedral, plays jazzy sounds until 4am and offers outdoor seating on the steps.

More handy for matchdays, **Café Montanha** and **Pastelaria Toledo** are both on Largo da Portagem, close to the bus stop for the stadium, with outdoor seats from where you can watch the world go by. Both offer everything from coffees and sandwiches to beer and wine; Montanha also does good pizzas.

For something more substantial, **Adega Paço do Conde**, Rua Paço do Conde 1, is a cavernous grill-house serving slabs of sizzling meat and fish at tables under a covered terrace, with worryingly cheap house wine. There are countless similar places in the maze of alleys between the town hall and the station.

More upbeat, **Via Latina** on Rua Almeida Garrett 1, close to Praça da República, keeps its punters dancing to techno until the small hours.

Venue verdict

The brand new, 32,000-seater **Estádio Calhabé** (also known as the Estádio Cidade da Coimbra) offers more than twice the capacity of its rundown predecessor, and lies just three kilometres southeast of the centre in a new sports park. The stadium is sleek and functional, though as it doubles as a municipal sports centre, complete with running track, the atmosphere for football matches looks sure to be diluted.

Buses #7, 11 and 24 head in the direction of the ground from opposite Largo da Portagem, passing the town hall on Rua Olimpio Nicolau Rui Fernandes. Tickets cost €1.30 on board, or you can buy three tickets for €1.47 in advance from central kiosks. Ask in the *turismo* for details of special buses that are likely to be laid on for matchdays; there is also plenty of underground parking for motorists.

Fixtures for the first round are **England v Switzerland** on 17 June and **Switzerland v France** on 21 June.

Faro

As the administrative regional capital of the Algarve, Faro is a substantial town ringed by tower blocks and urban sprawl. But its old centre is **extremely attractive**, made up of a series of whitewashed town houses set on winding cobbled alleys that lead down to a palm-lined marina. On the land side of marshy salt flats, there is no beach at Faro, but it is within easy striking distance of some offshore sandspit beaches – ferries depart from just south of the marina, below the old town walls.

Faro is also a short ride from some of the Algarve's **most popular resorts**: Vale de Lobo, Quarteira and Vilamoura are around 30 minutes' drive away, Albufeira around an hour. Beaches aside, there is plenty to keep you occupied in Faro, including a pretty Cidade Velha (the old walled town), some fine churches and a lively nightlife. The city's restaurants, too, are varied and better value than in the larger resorts.

The city's soccer team, **Farense**, have had spells in the top flight and were runners-up in the Portuguese cup in 1990, but although the best side in the Algarve, they currently languish in Portugal's *II Divisão*. Farense will share their new stadium with another second-division team from the neighbouring town of **Loulé**, 18km inland.

Getting there

Faro's airport is the **gateway to the Algarve's resorts**, and is well served by various scheduled and charter flights from all round the UK. From the airport, a free Aerobus runs hourly to the centre of town, a 15-minute ride. Slightly slower local buses #16 and #14 do the same run for €1, or take a taxi which will cost around €10. Faro's bus and train stations both lie just north of the centre – turn right and it is a minute's walk from the bus station to the marina, around five minutes' walk from the train station (turn right down Avenida da República).

Getting around

Faro is easy to explore on foot. The **tourist office** lies just outside the old town gates at Rua da Misericórdia 8 (daily 9.30am–12.30 & 1.30–5.30pm, ☎289 803 604) and has maps of the town and the area. For elsewhere in the Algarve, it is best to take one of the frequent buses from the main bus station – buy tickets in advance from the counters. Faro is also on the trans-Algarve train line, though local services are spectacularly slow. The line between the Algarve and Lisbon has been upgraded in time for the finals, obviating the need to take a ferry across the Tagus from Barreiro on arrival at the capital, and cutting journey times by up to a third.

Staying over

Faro is not overly endowed with hotels or guest houses, so rooms will be in short supply for Euro 2004. The town's smartest hotel is **Hotel Eva**, Avenida da República 1 (℡289 001 000), with marina-facing rooms and its own rooftop pool and restaurant. Doubles cost €115. **Residencial Algarve**, Rua Infante Dom Henriques 52 (℡289 895 700) is a spruce guest house well positioned near the train and bus stations. All rooms have TVs and private bath and the price of €90 a double includes breakfast. **Residencial Samé**, Rua do Bocage 66 (℡289 824 375), is another good option, with modern rooms, each with TV and private bathroom, from €75 for a double.

If you want to stay in style right on the beach, the five-star **Tivoli Marinotel** at nearby Vilamoura (℡289 303 303) has some 400 rooms, most with marina or sea views, and facilities include indoor and outdoor pools, but this will set you back €355 a double. Cheaper options can be had at the neighbouring, more downmarket resort of Quarteira, where the characterful **Pensão Miramar** on Rua Gonçalo Velho 8 (℡289 315 225) has spotless rooms, some with sea views and all with TVs and bath, for €50 a double including breakfast.

Another possibility is to camp: Faro's **cramped campsite** (℡289 817 876) lies on Praia de Faro, the town's nearest sandspit beach close the airport – phone ahead to check availability. Airport buses #14 and #16 both run out to the beach.

Alternatively, you could stay in **Loulé** which, though not by the sea, is only slightly further from the stadium than Faro itself. Check for availability with the tourist office (℡289 463 900) in advance. There are daily bus services between Loulé and Faro, Quarteira and Albufeira.

Eating, drinking and clubbing

Faro's university ensures it has a bouyant nightlife, during term-time at least. The liveliest bars are concentrated round the broad, pedestrianised Rua Conselheiro Bivar and the cobbled side streets parallel, Rua do Prior and Rua da Madalena. Things get lively after midnight, though **Upa Upa** at Rua Conselheiro Bivar 51 (closed Sundays) tends to fill up with a good time crowd by 10pm or so. The **Millenium III** nightclub at Rua do Prior 21 is the best bet for dance sounds until the small hours.

Faro has a large number of restaurants, most specialising in fish, seafood and grilled meats. **Sol e Jardim** at Praça Ferreira de Almeida 22–23 wins the quirky decor award, filled with flags, stuffed turtles and baskets, and jungle-like creepers over the patio roof. For bargain chicken and chips, try **Fim do Mundo**, Rua Vasco da Gama 53. To catch games on TV, **Café Piramides** on the marina-side Jardim Manuel Bivar, usually has screens showing matches in each corner of an all-purpose café serving everything from ice-creams and coffee to pizzas and beer.

The Algarve is littered with bars proudly displaying photos of famous footballers who have holidayed in the area (indeed, several have second homes here). In the nearby resort of Vilamoura, **Sete**, Bloco 7, Marina de Vilamoura is part-owned by

The Algarve Stadium is a joint venture between the city councils – and football teams – of Faro and Loulé

David Beckham's Real Madrid team-mate Luís Figo, and pictures on the walls show that many a soccer star has visited over the years. At other times, the fashionable steel and chrome café-bar offers karaoke sessions and a wide range of drinks.

Venue verdict

The **Algarve Stadium** is the only Euro 2004 arena to be built in a brand new area, well away from any previously existing football ground. It lies around 6km north of Faro between the main Faro–Loulé road and the IP1 motorway. Resembling giant, tented pavilions, the upper tiers are reached by spiral ramps that look as if they have been borrowed from a marble run; the highest seats have a superb if rather distant, birdseye view of the pitch.

The 30,000-capacity, all-seater stadium, which hosted England's friendly game against Portugal in February, can be reached by a **special bus service** during the competition; ask in the main EVA bus station on Avenida da República in Faro for details. Matches scheduled to be held here are **Spain v Russia** on 12 June and **Russia v Greece** on 20 June, along with the **quarter-final** between the winner of Group C and the runner-up in Group D, on 26 June.

Guimarães

Guimarães (pronounced 'gimmer-aysh') was the original Portuguese capital and birthplace of Afonso Henriques, the first king of Portugal after the conquest of the Moors. Today it is a provincial university town, but its **sense of history** is palpable and its centre was granted UNESCO World Heritage status in 2001.

The castle, ancient churches and labyrinth of streets certainly make this one of Portugal's **most alluring towns**. Guimarães' setting is likewise impressive, overlooked by the 617m-high mountain of Penha, the summit of which can be reached on a modern *Teleférico* cable car.

Vitória Guimarães, the town's football team, have rarely reached great heights, but are one of those northern teams that others fear to visit on a winter's evening. During the 1990s they were one of the strongest challengers to the big three of Porto, Sporting and Benfica, though they have failed to make much impact in recent seasons and last qualified for Europe in 1997.

Getting there

Guimarães is around 30 minutes' drive from Porto and Braga, and some 5.5 hours' drive from Lisbon. Regular trains from Porto take 1 hour 40 minutes. The **train station** is around a kilometre south of the centre – turn left from the station, and then right into Avenida Afonso Henriques. You'll see the **tourist office** on the right (Mon–Fri 9.30am–12.30pm & 2–6.30pm, ☎253 412 450), which can hand out maps of the town. The bus station is a little further out, around 15 minutes southwest of the centre. Turn right and head down Conde Margaride, then turn right at the market onto Rua Paio Galvão and you'll see the tourist office across the square, Largo do Toural.

Getting around

The old town's cobbled streets and squares are best explored on foot. From the tourist office it is a short walk north into the centre to **the main squares** of Praça de Santiago and Largo da Oliveira, around which you'll find most of the town's sites and its best student bars. North of here, it is a short walk down the picturesque Rua de Santa Maria to the town's imposing Castelo de São Miguel.

Staying over

Guimarães has a shortage of accommodation at the best of times and finding a room will be like discovering gold-dust during Euro 2004. **Albergaria das Palmeiras**

(☎ 253 410 324), in the shopping centre Centro Comercial das Palmeiras on Rua Gil Vicente, has modern, spotless rooms and its own parking facilities for €150 a double, which includes breakfast. **Hotel Residencial do Toural**, on Largo do Toural (entrance on Largo A L de Carvalho, ☎ 253 517 184) is a renovated town house with four-star comforts for €150 a double. If you can stretch to €200 for a double, **Hotel de Guimarães** (☎ 253 424 800) on Rua Dr Eduardo Almeida is a four-star place with its own garage parking, pool and health club.

Best budget option is **Pensão Imperial** (☎ 53 415 163), on Alameda São Damaso 111, which has basic but clean rooms with their own bathrooms for a bargain €30 a night. Finally, the nearest campsite, reached by cable car, lies on the slopes of Penha. The **Parque de Campismo da Penha** (☎ 253 515 912) even has its own pool.

Eating, drinking and clubbing

Guimarães has a lively nightlife, during term-time at least, with any number of bars round Largo da Oliveira and Praça de Santiago – **Carramão Arte Bar** at #33–35 of the latter square is a good bet. Most bars have tables spilling out onto the streets, perfect for people watching.

The most fashionable club is **Penha Clube**, by the bottom station of the cable car, which hosts occasional live bands. The town is also well-equipped with reasonably

The Estádio Dom Afonso Henriques has been refurbished rather than built from scratch – the shield at the entrance belongs to local club Vitória Guimarães

priced restaurants. **Adega dos Caquinhos** on Travessa da Arrochela means 'crockery wine-cellar' and serves solid Portuguese grills in a place with walls covered in brocken ceramics. **Café Oriental** on Largo do Toural is another good bet, with bargain Portuguese dishes including a local speciality, trout stuffed with ham.

Venue verdict

The **Estádio Dom Afonso Henriques** was completely remodelled in 2003 and now has an all-seater capacity of 30,000. The stadium is partly covered with four distinct stands on two levels, though seats at the top of the upper levels feel well back from the pitch. The stadium is around a 15-minute walk northwest from the centre – head to the main town market and take Rua de São Gonçalo. Fixtures for the tournament are **Denmark v Italy** on 14 June and **Italy v Bulgaria** on 22 June.

Leiria

Leiria had one of Portugal's first-ever printing presses, in 1480, and was the main royal abode for King Dinis during the early fourteenth century. The biggest thing to happen to the town since, however, is to host Euro 2004. Indeed, the Portuguese Association in Defence of the Siesta has its head-quarters in Leiria, which says a lot about this **sleepy town** in the Estremadura region of central Portugal. But, sat on the Rio Lis, the town's historic centre of cobbled streets and squares is an attractive ensemble. Though remodelled, the king's former home still overlooks the town in the form of a fairytale castle, one of the most impressive in Portugal

Leiria's other main attraction is its proximity to **some superb beaches** on the wild and wind-battered coast known as the Pinhal de Leiria – São Pedro de Muel in the most accessible, just 22 km to the west.

The town's football team, **União**, have held their own in the top division for several years now, and last season reached the Portuguese cup final.

Getting there

Leiria lies just off the **main A1 motorway** from Lisbon to Coimbra and Porto. Allow an hour and a half's drive here from Lisbon, half an hour from Coimbra and an hour and a half from Porto.

If travelling by public transport, it is best to get to Leiria by bus. The town's bus station is at the central Avenida Heróis de Angola, right by the Rio Lis and its riverside gardens, Jardim Luís de Camões. Buses to Leiria take between 1.5 and 2 hours from Lisbon and around an hour from Coimbra. Trains are far less convenient – they take 2–3 hours from Lisbon, and the station lies 4km north of the centre.

Getting around

Despite the inevitable high-rise sprawl of its suburbs, central Leiria is a manageable area easily negotiated on foot. The **tourist office** (daily 10am–1pm & 3–7pm, ☎244 814 748) is on Praça Goa, Dimão e Diu at the southern end of Jadrim Luís de Camões, and can give out maps and detail events round town.

The old town – and consequently the area of interest – spreads to the west and northwest, around Praça Rodrigues Lobo, Largo Mar Gomes da Cossa and Largo Cândido dos Reis. This steep network of streets extends to the Castelo, from where you get great views of the town – and the stadium to the northwest.

Staying over

Leiria is not geared up to mass tourism and consequently there is a shortage of accommodation. Even the humblest guest house has hiked its prices to take advantage of Euro 2004.

Residencial Dom Dinis, at Travessa de Tomar 2, east of the river, is very good value at €35 a double in a place with its own parking and roof terrace. The very central **Pensão Alcôa**, Rua Rodrigues Cordeiro 24–26 (☎244 832 690) offers small rooms, but they all come with bath and TVs and the €70 a double includes breakfast in the downstairs restaurant, which does decent Portuguese food throughout the day. A little south of the centre, close to the riverside Largo Alexandro Herculano, **Residencial Ramalhete** at Rua Dr Correia Mateus 30 (☎244 812 802) is overpriced at €100 a double, but this does include breakfast and all rooms have private bathrooms and TVs.

If you have no luck in Leiria itself, there is usually plenty of accommodation to be had in the town of **Fátima**, 25 minutes' bus ride from Leiria. Rowdy football crowds will not be viewed sympathetically as this is one of the main pilgrimage destinations for the Portuguese, but that does mean the town is geared up for huge numbers of visitors for the principal pilgrimages in May and October. **Irmãs Dominicanos**, on Rua Francisco Marto 50 (☎249 533 317), has doubles from €37.50 in an attractive old building near the main square.

Another option is to camp – there are several campsites on the Pinhal de Leiria coast, some 20km west of Leiria. The site at the attractive seaside resort of **São Pedro de Muel** (☎244 599 168) is crowded but most convenient for Leiria, though without a car you may need to change buses in the town of Marinha Grande.

Eating, drinking and clubbing

Leiria does not quite make the premier league in terms of nightlife, although the bars and cafés along Largo Cândido dos Reis do get lively on a warm summer's evening.

Bar Estrebaria at #23 is a good place to start, while later action takes places at the club **Xannax**, at Rua Mouzinho de Albuquerque 168, northwest of the bus station on the way to the stadium.

Pastelaria Arcadia is a fine breakfast stop on the arcaded Praça Rodrigues Lobo, while **Café Restaurante Esplanada de Leiria** does substantial buffet meals by the main gardens, Jardim Luís de Camões.

For a full meal, **Restaurante Cervejaria Camões**, also on Jardim Luís de Camões, does inexpensive Portuguese cuisine with tables overlooking the river and park (closed Mondays), and has a dance club, **Sabor Latino**, on its first floor. For bargain grills, head to **Restaurante Montecarlo**, on Rua Dr Correia Mateus, south of the riverside Largo Alexandro Herculano.

Venue verdict

The **Estádio Dr Magalhães Pessoa** (also known as the Estádio Municipal) is home to União Leiria and was upgraded in 2003 to seat 30,000 spectators, most under cover. This is the third stadium designed by leading architect Tomás Taveira, who also worked on the new stadia of Sporting Lisbon and Beira-Mar of Aveiro.

Unlike his other arenas, this one incorporates an athletics track which – though rated the best in Portugal – inevitably removes the spectators from the action to a degree. Nevertheless, the sleek roof and smooth lines make it an impressive stadium which lies just ten minutes' walk northwest from the centre. The fixture schedule here is **Switzerland v Croatia** on 13 June and **Croatia v France** on 17 June.

Award-winning architect Tomás Taveira has given Leiria's stadium his trademark colour and eccentricity

Lisbon

Hosting matches at all stages of the competition, including the final on 4 July, Lisbon is within easy striking distance of all the other venues – the furthest, Braga, is less than 400 kilometres away. Not surprisingly, many of the teams, including England, have chosen Lisbon as their **permanent base** for Euro 2004.

Many fans will probably follow suit, as the capital and its surroundings also offer a wide range of affordable accommodation. In fact the cultural and intellectual heart of the country pretty much has it all, with a world-class art collection at the Gulbenkian Foundation, a ruined Moorish castle offering tremendous views over the city, a **pulsating nightlife**, and a cost of living that is one of the lowest in the EU.

Add to that a fleet of superbly eccentric forms of transport, a highly atmospheric street life, a balmy climate and proximity to some stunning **Atlantic beaches**, and it is a wonder that Lisbon is not better known as a holiday destination in its own right.

As a further bonus, June also sees various festivals in the capital, including the *Rock-in-Rio* rock festival, which features international bands and an estimated 100,000 visitors for the week leading up to Euro 2004. A little later, the city's main street festival for *Santo António* on 12–13 June sees all-night partying in the Alfama district, while *Luzboa* is a one-off festival of light festival, with installations at the Miradouro São Pedro de Alcântara in the Bairro Alto.

Despite all this, Lisbon is probably best known for its football teams, Benfica and Sporting, who dominate the Portuguese club scene along with Porto. **Benfica** are traditionally the bigger team, having won the European Cup in 1962 and been runners-up on three other occasions, but in recent years they have run up against the buffers of a financial crisis and now look back fondly on the days when Sven-Göran Eriksson guided them to domestic and European success in the early 1990s.

Nowadays, city rivals **Sporting** are more successful, having won the domestic title twice since the new millennium. They have close links with Manchester United – Peter Schmeichel played here after leaving Old Trafford, and erstwhile assistant coach Carlos Queiroz was an ex-Sporting boss. The relationship helped the English club land wonderkid Cristiano Ronaldo in 2003.

Getting there

Lisbon's **airport** is right on the edge of the city, which means a taxi into the centre costs only €12–15. Alternatively, a regular Aerobus (€2.50, free to TAP passengers) runs to the centre every 20 minutes. Local buses #44 and #45 do the same run for €1, but with more frequent stops and less room for baggage.

Train services from the north of Portugal and Spain terminate at Santa Apolónia station, on the riverfront a kilometre east of the centre – take a taxi or any bus heading west from there to the central Praça do Comércio. From the Algarve, slow trains terminate south of the Tejo (Tagus) river at Barreiro, which means catching a ferry (free to train ticket holders) to Praça do Comércio. Trains using the new fast line terminate at Oriente station, east of the centre at the Parque das Nações, on the Oriente metro line.

Lisbon's main **bus terminal** is in the north of the city close to Saldanha metro, some 15 minutes from the centre by underground.

Wrought-iron gates from Sporting's old stadium adorn the walls of the new one

Though the city is well served by Portugal's **motorway network**, driving in Lisbon itself is a nightmare, with frequent jams, hair-raising junctions and a paucity of parking spaces. If you've rented a car or brought your own, leave it on the outskirts.

Getting around

Central Lisbon is fairly compact, but as it is built on seven hills, you will probably want to use public transport to save some steep climbs and to see the outlying sights. And at just €2.75 for a **one-day travel pass**, valid on the metro, buses, trams and street lifts, public transport is extremely good value. Passes are obtained from various kiosks round town, which also sell bus and tram tickets in advance for €1 (valid for two journeys); this is cheaper than the tickets purchased onboard which cost the same for one ride.

Lisbon's efficient and modern **metro** is the best way to reach the football stadia and many sites such as the Gulbenkian. Flat-fare tickets cost €0.65, though a book of ten tickets costs just €5.10.

Finally, **taxis** are also inexpensive, especially if shared between a group. An average ride across town costs around €7.

Staying over

Lisbon is far more geared to visitors than any other host city in Portugal, but even so, accommodation will still be hard to come by and correspondingly over-priced during Euro 2004. In the heart of the central Baixa district, **Residencial Insulana**, Rua da Assunção (☎213 423 131) is a good place to start, with smart rooms and its own bar from €65 a double. Two more basic options, also in the Baixa, are **Pensão Prata**, Rua da Prata 71 (☎213 468 908), a family-run pension with spartan but clean doubles from €40 (some with their own shower rooms), and **Pensão Coimbra e Madrid**, on the central (and noisy) Praça da Figueira 3 (☎213 424 808), where rooms (with or without bath) come at €40 a double.

A little further out, but overlooking Lisbon's main park, **Hotel Miraparque**, Avenida Sidónio Pais 12 (☎213 524 286), is a good old-fashioned hotel with its own bar and restaurant (and TVs in the room for live games) from €150 a double. Further out still, but close to the lively docks area, **Barco do Tejo**, Travessa do Cruz da Rocha 3 (☎213 977 055) is a clean and pleasant pension run by characterful characters, and as it is off the beaten track is more likely to have rooms.

Another option is to camp. The city's main campsite, **Parque Municipal de Campismo** (☎217 623 100) is in the Parque Florestal de Monsanto, a substantial park 6km to the west of the centre. The site has its own pool and shops, but allow a good 30-minute bus ride to get there on #43 from Praça da Figueira.

Eating, drinking and clubbing

The city has the whole gamut of restaurants, from swanky international haunts at the redeveloped docks to local eateries where three courses will cost under €10. Fish and seafood are the specialities, and the central pedestrianised Rua das Portas de Santo Antão is famed for its seafood restaurants – **Solmar**, at #108, is cavernous enough to feed most of a football stadium. **Bom Jardim** at nearby Travessa de Santo Antão is renowned for its grilled chicken, with outside seats from which to watch the world go by.

Another area laced with restaurants is the Bairro Alto, the best place in town to go drinking and clubbing. Take your pick from hundreds of small bars that get going after midnight in a warren of narrow streets that become livelier as the night progresses. Hardened clubbers should head to Santa Apolónia, where **Lux** (Cais da Pedra a Santa Apolónia), part-owned by actor John Malkovich, attracts a mixed

The design of the red-edged Estádio da Luz is a modern re-interpretation of Benfica's famous, vast original

crowd as well as top-name DJs and bands. This club has done more than any to put Lisbon on the international clubbing map, though others – such as **Fragil** at Rua da Atalaia 126 in the Bairro Alto and **Kremlin** at Escadinhas da Praia 5 in the Santo district – can be just as much fun.

Venue verdict

Lisbon's two state-of-the-art Euro 2004 stadia are a short drive apart on the 2nd Circular, the city's equivalent of London's North Circular Road. Near the airport, Sporting's **Estádio José Alvalade** is a stunning green spaceship designed by leading Portuguese architect Tomás Taveira.

The arena has been built adjacent to Sporting's original stadium, which bore the same name, and its exterior is completely tiled in Sporting's colours and propped up by giant ship-like masts. The stadium's underbelly embraces restaurants, bars, cinemas and even a bowling alley, while the interior seats 52,000.

To reach the Alvalade, take the metro to Campo Grande on the Girassol or Caravela lines. Better than the bars in the stadium itself is **Pastelaria Dourada**, on

Rua Cipriano Dourado right by the ground. This bustling café-bar serves everything from beer to coffees, pizzas and sandwiches, and you'll have locals for company.

The Alvalade is due to host five games during Euro 2004. At the group stage, there's **Sweden v Bulgaria** on 14 June, **Spain v Portugal** on 20 June and **Germany v Czech Republic** on 23 June. After that there'll be the **quarter-final** between the winners of Group B and the runners-up in Group A on 25 June, followed by the first **semi-final** on 30 June.

Though the Estádio Alvalade is superb, the brand new **Estádio da Luz** to the west surpasses it. Benfica's new home, adjacent to the former stadium of the same name, has been built in a style similar to the famous original, which was dubbed the 'cathedral'. (The English interpretation of the Portuguese name, 'Stadium of Light', stems from a misunderstanding. Although 'Luz' means 'light' in Portuguese, the name actually refers to the Lisbon suburb of Luz, in which the ground is located.) Resembling a red-edged crown, the new stadium holds 65,000. To get there, take the metro to Colégio Militar/Luz on the Gaivota line.

Don't be alarmed when you find the metro exits into a shopping centre, **Colombo**. The stadium is well signposted, but if you fancy exploring one of Europe's biggest shopping malls first, allow plenty of time as there are more than 400 shops, 65 restaurants and the Fun Centre – the largest indoor amusement park in Europe, complete with go-kart track, ten-pin bowling and even a rollercoaster.

Luz will host **France v England** on 13 June, **Russia v Portugal** on 16 June and **Croatia v England** on 21 June. After that there'll be the **quarter-final** between the winners of Group A and the runners-up in Group B on 24 June, before Portugal says farewell to the European Championship at **the final itself** on 4 July.

Porto

A UNESCO World Heritage Site, central Porto is an extraordinary cityscape of densely packed houses, shops and churches spilling down the precipitous valleyside of the Douro river. Famed for its port wine lodges – which actually lie south of the river in the suburb of Vila Nova de Gaia – Porto is the only place in Portugal outside the capital with a big-city feel. It boasts a spanking new metro and a daily bustle that marks it out as the country's **economic powerhouse**. The saying goes that Porto works while Lisbon plays, but these gritty northerners – known as *tripeiros*, tripe-eaters, after the local dish – are also famously friendly.

There is an edge to the city, however, and as Manchester United fans found to their cost in 1997, the local police do not treat troublemakers with velvet gloves. United reacquainted themselves with **FC Porto** in last season's Champions League, and Porto have been by far the most successful team in the country over the last fifteen years. In 2003 they beat Celtic to win the UEFA Cup, and in José Mourinho they have one of Europe's most highly rated coaches. Having offloaded their promising young striker Hélder Postiga to Tottenham, their current star player is Deco, a Brazilian-raised Portuguese international and playmaker.

Porto's second team, **Boavista**, shocked the nation by winning the Portuguese championship in 2001 – the only team outside the 'big three' of Sporting, Benfica and Porto to win it in over 50 years. Since then, after a brief flirtation with Champions League football, they have slipped back to their customary upper- to mid- table position. Their most famous former player is Dutchman Jimmy Floyd Hasselbaink, who played here under the nickname 'Jimmy' until Leeds United brought him to the Premiership.

Getting there

Scheduled flights from the UK (mostly from Heathrow and Gatwick) serve Porto's **international airport**, which lies 13km north of the city. Regular buses #56 and #87 make the 30–40 minute run into town. If you fly with TAP, you can use a free Aerobus service direct to most hotels; other passangers pay €2.50. Taxis cost around

Porto's new Dragão stadium has an efficient, businesslike air about it – much like the city itself

€15. Porto's São Bento **train station** lies right in the heart of the city – turn right and it is a minute's walk to Avenida dos Aliados, the main square. Alfa trains connect Porto with Lisbon (3.5 hours) via Coimbra (1.5 hours) and Aveiro (1 hour).

Buses use various terminals around town, the most central being on Rua Entreparedes, near Praça da Batalha, five minutes east of Avenida dos Aliados. From here there are regular services to Braga (1 hour 20 minutes) and Guimarães (2 hours). **Motorists** should avoid Porto's narrow, traffic-ridden central streets if at all possible (except on a Sunday when the streets are quiet). Allow 3 hours' drive time from Lisbon, 45 minutes from Aveiro, Guimarães and Braga, and a good 5 hours from Faro.

Getting around

Despite Porto's riverside sprawl, the central area is small enough to see on foot. There is also a comprehensive local **bus network** – route maps are available from the tourist offices – and as elsewhere in Portugal, tickets are cheaper if you buy them in advance (€0.70 a ticket) from kiosks or newsagents than if you buy them onboard the bus itself (€1.20).

Porto also has two **tram routes**, which trundle out along the river – not a particularly useful service but worth experiencing for fun at €0.50 a ride. Taxis are also inexpensive. Finally, the first part of Porto's long-awaited **metro system** is up and running, with useful stops at Campanha rail station, Trindade (at the top of the central square) and Porto's stadium (see below). Single tickets cost €0.80 in the central zone.

The main **tourist office** lies on Rua Clube Fenianos 25 close to Trindade metro at the north-west end of Avenida dos Aliados (daily 9am-7pm, ☎223 393 470).

Staying over

Despite its size, Porto will be full to the gills during Euro 2004 and accommodation will be in short supply. Most of the inexpensive accommodation is to be found in tall tenement buildings on and around Avenida dos Aliados.

Pensão Pão de Açucar, Rua do Almada 262 (☎222 002 425) has a mixed bag of rooms, all with their own private bathrooms, from €60 a double. **Grande Hotel de Paris**, Rua da Fábrica 27–29 (☎222 073 140) is a characterful central hotel with bright rooms – each with bath and TV – grouped round an internal balcony. Doubles cost €80. A little further out, but more likely to have rooms, is the rambling **Pensão do Norte**, Rua de Fernandes Tomás 579 (☎222 003 503). Some rooms have private bathrooms and balconies overlooking the street, and start at a bargain €20 a double.

Porto's main campsite is at Prelada, 3km north-west of the centre, on the same side of town as the Estádio do Bessa. The **Parque de Campismo da Prelada** (☎228 312 616) can be reached by city buses #54 (from Cordoaria) and #6 (from Avenida dos Aliados).

Eating, drinking and clubbing

Virtually every worker in Porto seems to go out for a substantial lunch, probably as set meals in the day can be astonishingly cheap – as low as €5 for three courses including wine in some establishments.

More salubrious places are to be found on and around Cais da Ribeira, the main riverside drag – the liveliest place to head for a meal or a drink. Here, **A Canastra** on Cais da Ribeira 37 serves solid Portuguese dishes at sensible prices. A little away from the river, but still with river views, **Restaurante O Gancho** on Largo do Terreiro 9–10 serves inexpensive fish, meat and omelettes with outdoor tables. **Miradouro**, on the top of the arches of Cais da Ribeira near the bridge, is more of a bar but does bargain pizzas, steak sandwiches and salads as well as serving cheap beer.

In the centre of town, **Regaleira**, on Rua do Bonjardim near Praça Dom João I, has pretensions to be upmarket, with quality fish and seafood, but isn't above having a TV on above the bar showing live football.

Boavista's distinctive checker-board shirts are reflected in the seating at Bessa

For nightlife, the narrow alleys around Cais da Ribeira are the best places to explore, especially Rua da Fonte Tourina. **Está-Se Bem** (closed Sunday) at #70–72 attracts an arty crowd until 2am, while **Ribeira Negra** at #66–68 is popular with a heavy-drinking, studenty crowd.

A visit to the **port wine lodges** over the river in Vila Nova da Gaia is also a must. Tours all include a free tasting, and while you're over here, check out **Hard Club**, on the riverfront Cais de Gaia, one of the city's main venues for visiting DJs and occasional live music.

Venue verdict

Porto's two stadiums lie at either end of town to the north of the centre and have a very different feel. In the north-east of the city in the residential district of Antas, the brand new **Estádio Dragão** (Dragon Stadium) was built alongside the old Antas ground and forms the focal point of a new urban regeneration project featuring a conference centre, shopping mall and leisure complex. Holding 52,000 and home to FC Porto, the stadium is all clean lines and sweeping views. To get here, take bus #6, #49, #59 or #78 from Rua de Sá da Bendeira, near the Bolhão market, or take the blue metro line to Estádio do Dragão (single fare €1).

The Dragão will host the tournament's **opening ceremony** and its inaugural fixture of **Portugal v Greece** on 12 June. After that there's **Germany v Holland** on 15 June, **Italy v Sweden** on 18 June, the **quarter-final** between the winner of Group D and the runner-up in Group C on 27 June, and the second **semi-final** on 1 July.

To the north-west of the centre, the **Estádio do Bessa** is the substantially reconstructed home of Boavista, which now incorporates a sports complex complete with gymnasium, tennis courts and training grounds. With a combined capacity of 30,000, the stands are compact and close to the pitch, giving an intimate air familiar to smaller Premiership and Nationwide League teams in England.

To get here, take bus #3 from Praça da Liberdade, at the bottom of Avenida dos Aliados, or bus #24 or #41 from Jardim da Cordoaria. Check also with the local **tourist offices** for details of special bus services that are likely to be laid on during Euro 2004 matchdays. Bessa will host three first-round fixtures: **Greece v Spain** on 16 June, **Latvia v Germany** on 19 June and **Denmark v Sweden** on 22 June.

Fans, food, history, statistics and more...

The Context

National culture

Tourists who arrive in Portugal overland from Spain are immediately struck by how **different the country feels**. Where the Spaniards are bositerous and exuberant, the Portuguese have a tendency to be quieter and more discreet. While Spanish food may drip with oil, the Portuguese prefer their meals more simply prepared. And while Spanish and Portuguese may look very similar as languages on paper, in conversation they sound quite different, the latter complicated by all sorts of weird, gutteral noises that are supposed to pass for vowels.

Not that Portugal is a homogenous land. Though only about the size of Scotland, it is twice as densely populated, and in terms of population and of customs, differences between **the north and the south** can be striking. Above a line more or less corresponding with the course of the River Tagus (Tejo in Portuguese), the indigenous people are of predominantly Celtic and Germanic stock. It was here, at Guimarães, that the 'Lusitanian' nation was born, in the wake of the Christian reconquest from the North African Moors.

South of the Tagus, where the Moorish and Roman civilisations were most established, people are darker-skinned and maintain more of the 'Mediterranean' lifestyle that will be familiar to travellers with experience of Spain.

More recent events are woven into the pattern. Portugal's 1974 revolution came from the south – an area of vast estates, rich landowners and a dependent workforce – while the **conservative backlash** of the 1980s had its roots in the north, with its powerful religious authorities and individual smallholders wary of change.

More profoundly even than revolution, **emigration** has altered people's attitudes and the appearance of the countryside. After Lisbon, the largest Portuguese community is in Paris, and there are migrant workers spread throughout France and Germany. Returning to Portugal, these emigrants have brought in modern ideas and challenged many traditional rural values.

The greatest of all Portuguese influences, however, is **the sea**. The Portuguese are very conscious of themselves as a seafaring race; mariners like Vasco da Gama led the way in the exploration of Africa and the Americas, and until less than 30 years ago Portugal remained a colonial power. The colonies brought African and South American strands to the country's culture, notably in the distinctive music of *fado* – sentimental songs heard in Lisbon, Coimbra and elsewhere – and, of course, in the country's football.

Practicalities

Citizens of the European Union need have only a **valid passport** to enter Portugal, and can stay indefinitely. Currently citizens of the US, Canada, Australia and New Zealand can also enter and stay for up to 90 days with just a passport, but visa requirements do change, so check the situation before you leave.

Portugal is one of the 12 European Union countries which have joined the **single European currency**, the euro (€). Your best bet for cheap exchange is to use a credit or bank card at a cash machine; commission on travellers' cheques can be high. Banking hours are Mon–Fri 8.30am–3pm; in Lisbon and in some of the Algarve resorts counters may be open in the evening to change money.

Credit and debit cards are widely accepted, but note that if you have a Cirrus card (such as Switch in the UK), you will have to enter your four-digit PIN to make a purchase in a shop or restaurant, as well as to get cash out of a hole in the wall. Visa and Mastercard users would be well-advised to memorise their PINs before they leave home as well, since their usage is spreading as a means of combating fraud.

Essential vocabulary

Hello *Olá*
Goodbye *Adeus*
Yes *Sim*
No *Não*
Two beers, please *Duas cervejas, por favor*
Thank you *Obrigado (said by men)/Obrigada (said by women)*
Men's toilets *Homens*
Women's toilets *Senhoras*
Where is the stadium? *Onde esta o estádio?*
Entrance *Entrada*
Exit *Saída*
What's the score? *Como esta o jogo?*
Score a goal *Marcar um gol*
Referee *Árbitro*
Offside *Fora de jogo*

Getting around

Most **trains** in Portugal, run by the state operator CP, are classed as *regional* – they're cheap but stop everywhere. Faster and more expensive are the *intercidades*, while the fastest of all are the *rápidos*, such as the Alfa service which runs between Lisbon and Porto. There are four Alfas a day and the journey takes just over three hours. For more information on times and fares, check out the CP website which has English versions of most of its pages: Ⓦ **www.cp.pt**.

Buses can be a good alternative to trains – the network is more extensive and fares are competitive. In contrast to rail services, however, most major inter-city bus routes are run by private companies, and information on times and fares can be hard to come by.

Car rental rates are among Europe's lowest, but petrol (*gasolina*) is relatively expensive. Most cars will run on unleaded (*sem chumbo*) petrol. Driving licences

A beer, an outside table and the day's football papers – all, tragically, part of daily life in Portugal's towns and cities

from EU countries are accepted, even if they are not of the EU standard type. If you're from outside the EU, you will need an international driving licence.

Eating and drinking

Portuguese food is not always the most sophisticated, but it is **good value** and served in quantity. Indeed, you can often have a substantial meal by ordering a half portion (*meia dose*), or a portion (*uma dose*) between two.

Apart from straightforward *resturantes*, you could find yourself eating a meal in one of several other venues. A *tasca* is a small, neighbourhood tavern; a *casa de pasto* is a local dining room usually serving a **set three-course meal** (*ementa turística*), often at lunchtime only. A *cervejaria* is literally a 'beer house', more informal than a restaurant, with people dropping in at all hours for a beer and a snack. A *churrascaria* is a restaurant specialising in grilled meat and fish, while a *marisqueria* will have a superior fishy menu, with the emphasis on seafood.

Meal times are usually noon–3pm for lunch, with dinner from 7.30pm onwards; don't count on being able to eat much after 11pm.

Portuguese beer (*cerveja*) is limited to three major brands: Sagres, Super Bock and Cristal. All are extremely drinkable pilsener-style beers, and all are also available as dark lagers which can be strangely refreshing. When drinking draft beer, order *um imperial* if you want a regular glass; *uma caneca* will get you a half-litre.

Football culture

To sit alongside the Portuguese as they watch a big football game can be an education in itself. Their support is passionate, their chanting fervent, their applause generous. But what marks them out is that every single one of them appears to be **'living' the game**. The action is accompanied by constant murmurings as each fan tries to envision what should happen next – who the ball should be moved on to, how, and when.

These are not the pointless exclamations of fans urging their heroes to "have a dig" or "get rid". For one thing, they are too quiet for the players to hear. But though they may not be loud, they say a lot about how Portugal views its football – as **a serious pastime** to be appreciated with care, in contrast to the hysteria that sometimes prevails in neighbouring Spain, for example.

Many Portuguese footballers begin learning their craft playing an indoor version of the game, *Futebol de Salão*. As in 5-a-side football in Britain, the ball is not allowed to go **over head height** and the goalkeeper's 'D' zone is a no-go area for outfield players. Unlike British 5-a-side, the Portuguese organise leagues and other competitions which come close to equalling the 11-a-side game in status and celebrity.

As well as explaining the fans' intimate appreciation of a footballer's skill, the fascination with the indoor game inevitably influences the development of 11-a-side professionals. It helps to explain why, for example, Portuguese players generally have **excellent close control**, and why so many teams – both domestically and internationally – have tended to lack a big, physical presence, particularly in attack.

Portuguese fans also appreciate other styles of football, however, and the welcome that will be extended to all nationalities during Euro 2004 will stem in part from an eagerness to explore and experience different ways of playing, and watching, the beautiful game.

Match practice

Recent crowd trouble at a game between Boavista and Guimarães and the tragic on-field death of a Benfica player show that Portuguese soccer is not immune to **bad publicity**. But on the whole a Portuguese football match is laid back and family orientated, with hardcore hooligans and criminal behaviour restricted to a distinct minority. For Euro 2004, the organisers hope to promote the festival-like atmosphere usually to be found at big club games in Portugal, and have pledged to provide **low-profile policing** despite tight behind-the-scenes security measures.

England's February friendly against Portugal in the Algarve passed off entirely without incident – a tribute to the effectiveness of the authorities' approach, as well as to the friendliness of the locals.

A football-mad nation at the best of times, the Portuguese have embraced the hype surrounding Euro 2004 with an almost naïve enthusiasm. The domestic game has already witnessed a version of the 'rugby effect' seen in England after the last Rugby World Cup. People who have never taken an interest in football before are **suddenly hooked**, and attendances for league games have soared, especially at clubs whose stadia are hosting Euro 2004 fixtures.

All this is perhaps just as well, since during the tournament it will be **hard to avoid football** wherever you are in Portugal. Virtually every café and bar, not to mention most restaurants, will be showing games on TV in one corner or other, while in public spaces such as parks or street corners, elderly men will be huddled on benches with radios pressed to their ears.

Watching Portugal play inside the stadia – or even on television – is sure to be an experience, although at times the seriousness with which the Portuguese take their football can **border on the depressive**. Even when their team is winning, the slightest incident will force grown men to indulge in theatrical groaning, or hang their heads in shame

A popular insult is *'Ai, que frango flagrante!'* – literally, 'what a flagrant chicken!' – used when a goalkeeper commits a handling error. At other times the referee will be the subject of abuse, inspiring chants of *'Gatuno!'* – 'Bandit!' As in Spain, an outbreak of **waving of white hankies** inside the ground (a custom inherited from bullfights) can signal either appreciation of an outstanding piece of play, or dissatisfaction at a below-par performance.

Portugal on the net

Ⓦ **www.portugal.org**
Official website of the Portuguese tourist office

Ⓦ **www.portugalvirtual.pt**
Directory of everything from hotels to shops, tourist sites and culture

Ⓦ **www.maisturismo.pt**
Search engine for hotels, mostly at the upper end of the market

Ⓦ **www.min-cultura.pt**
Ministry of Culture's website, with details of events in major towns

Catering corner

Loud Latin rhythms and stalls outside the grounds promote the festival-like atmosphere of Portuguese games, as do the **steaming concessions vans** offering hot and cold snacks. Though they can be hard to distinguish from one another amid the smoke, *bifanas* are pork steak sandwiches, *entremeadas* are fatty pork sandwiches and *pregos* beef sandwiches. None should set you back more than €3.

Alcohol is not sold inside grounds, so fans are generally assaulted by beer and wine sellers at the entrance – whether these survive the increased levels of security at Euro 2004 remains to be seen. If you want to avoid the branded food of tournament sponsors, **traditional local snacks** come in the form of peanuts (*amendoins torrados*), pickled lupin seeds (*tremoços*) and sweet cakes such as *queijadas*.

Action replay

The opening game, the final and many of the group games will be shown live on Portugal's main RTP channel, with some games also shown on SIC and the satellite channel TV1. With live games being broadcast in **virtually every bar** and café in the country, and with most half-decent hotels offering global satellite or cable TV channels, it should not be hard to catch the live game of your choice. All the national newspapers carry **TV listings**, as do the weekly listings magazines *TV Guia*, *TV Mais* and *TV 7 Dias*.

The back page

The day's leading British and **international newspapers** usually make the main central newsstands and hotel lobbies at some stage in Lisbon, Faro and Porto, though it's usually the next day before they make it to elsewhere in the country.

Portugal's newspapers will all give prominent coverage to Euro 2004 while the tournament is on, and though in Portuguese only, all have stats and facts that are easy to decipher. *O Público* and *O Diário de Notícias* are the two leading broadsheets with substantial sports sections.

Portugal's leading **sports paper** is Lisbon's well-established *A Bola* (daily, online version at ⓦ**www.abola.pt**), which devotes something like 90% of its coverage to football. Although only in Portuguese and with a bias towards domestic soccer gossip, is also has extensive coverage of the international game.

There are two other sports dailies. *O Jogo* (ⓦ**www.ojogo.pt**) publishes separate Lisbon and Porto editions, and is therefore more popular in the north, while the slightly downmarket *Record* is the paper to have lifted the lid on most of the Portuguese game's recent scandals.

In the net

The main **tournament website** is the official one at ⓦ**www.euro2004.com**, with comprehensive information on fixtures, ventures and, of course, all the teams. It is particularly strong on news content, with seemingly every little injury to even the most insignificant squad player being reported on. The **Portuguese FA** runs a very well-maintained and very comprehensive official website at (ⓦ**www.fpf.pt**) which also covers Euro 2004, though in Portuguese only.

The best site in English for information on both the **Portuguese domestic game** and international news is ⓦ**www.portuguesesoccer.com**, which has news, scores and links to various other football sites, including links to most Portuguese league teams' official homepages.

Tournament history

It is a measure of just how far the European Championship has come that the two nations which took part in its first final in 1960 no longer exist. It is 46 years since the qualifying rounds for the 'European Nations Cup' kicked off with a preliminary-round tie between Ireland and Czechoslovakia (another of Europe's former nation states), and in that time the event has gone on to become the **third most important** in the global sporting calendar, after the World Cup and the summer Olympic Games.

What follows is an overview of how each edition of the tournament has unfolded – the key players, coaches, goals and near-misses that have thrilled a continent, and which continue to inspire today's generation of players, coaches, administrators and supporters…

First edition: 1960

After a Frenchman, Henri Delaunay, first proposed the idea of a European Championship in the mid-1950s, the inaugural competition kicked off on 5 April 1958. The event was initially known as the **European Nations Cup**. Delaunay died before the tournament got underway and the trophy was named after him. Despite the established appeal of the World Cup, some national FAs were sceptical about the new event, and absentees from the first edition included Italy, West Germany and all four 'home' nations: England, Scotland, Wales and Northern Ireland. The tournament's final stages (semi-finals onwards) were hosted by the French, who surprisingly lost their semi 5–4 to Yugoslavia in Paris, after conceding three goals in four second-half minutes. The Yugoslavs in turn were beaten 2–1 by the Soviet Union after extra time in the final, the Soviets' hero being goalkeeper Lev Yashin.

> ### King Arthur
>
> *The first final was played at the Parc des Princes, Paris, and refereed by an Englishman, **Arthur Ellis**, who would later find fame if no great fortune as the adjudicator on the 1970s BBC TV show 'It's A Knockout'*

Franco's U-turn: 1964

All the home nations except Scotland were persuaded to enter but the tournament was still a relatively lightweight affair, with a straight knockout format rather than qualifying groups. Among the odder results were **Luxembourg's defeat of Holland** and Albania's walk over Greece, who refused to play them for political reasons. Holders the Soviet Union again progressed all the way to the final, but this time they were beaten 2–1 by Spain in Madrid, in front of dictator General Franco who had refused his side permission to travel to play the same opponents four years earlier.

Grouped together: 1968

Qualifying groups were used for the first time as the tournament continued to expand. England made their best progress to date, losing 1–0 to Yugoslavia in the semi-finals in Florence after Alan Mullery had become the **first man ever to be sent off** while wearing an England shirt. The Yugoslavs then lost a replayed final 2–0 to Italy after the latter were awarded a controversial free-kick equaliser in the first game. Only two days' break were allowed between the first match and the replay, during which the Italians were able to call up five new players while Yugoslavia had only a single substitute at their disposal.

'Der Bomber' in Brussels: 1972

West Germany swept all before them in what was only the second European Championship they had ever entered. England were beaten 3–1 at Wembley in the quarter-finals, the visitors' Gunter Netzer **running rings around Alf Ramsey's defence**. Belgium hosted the final stages but the local population didn't exactly get bitten by football fever: only 2,000 souls turned up to see the Soviet Union beat Hungary 1–0 in the second semi-final in Brussels.

Luck of the Lira

When Italy captain **Giacinto Facchetti** *lifted the trophy in Rome in 1968, it was in the knowledge that his team had only reached the final after beating the Soviet Union on the toss of a coin in the semis*

In the first, the hosts went down 2–0 to the Germans, for whom Gerd 'der Bomber' Müller got both goals. In the final, the Soviets suffered a similar fate, Müller grabbing another brace in a 3–0 win.

Belgrade beauty: 1976

The last finals to consist solely of knockout games are considered to be a classic of their era. All four semis went to extra time and no team failed to score in any game, as the 'total football' of Holland and West Germany came up against the canny counter-attacking of Czechoslovakia and hosts Yugoslavia. In the first semi, the Czechs, who had eliminated Don Revie's England in the qualifiers, beat Johan Cruyff's Holland 3–1 after extra time, in a game dominated by Welsh referee Clive Thomas, who sent-off three players. In the other match, the Germans came back from 2–0 down to eliminate Yugoslavia with typical resilience – Dieter Müller, no relation to Gerd, was **the villain of the piece** for the 70,000 fans at the Red Star stadium in Belgrade, scoring a hat-trick in a 4–2 win.

In the final, West Germany returned to the same stadium and clawed back another two-goal deficit against Czechoslovakia with a last-minute equaliser by Bernd Hölzenbein. But the Czechs held firm in extra time and the match went to penalties. All were scored until Uli Hoeness skied his effort over the bar, leaving Czechoslovakia's Antonín Panenka with the opportunity to lob the ball cheekily into an empty goal while German 'keeper Sepp Maier dived in vain.

Frustration and fog: 1980

The Italians played host for the second time, as UEFA expanded the final stages to eight teams, arranged in two groups of four. Clumsily, however, the competition was given no semi-final stage, meaning that the two group winners went straight through to the final. The arrangement frustrated good football and infuriated fans, contributing to the **worst scenes of hooliganism** yet seen at a European Championship. Police used teargas as England were held 1–1 by Belgium, and several players had to be treated by doctors after collapsing in the noxious fog. Marco Tardelli then effectively ended England's tournament by scoring the only goal of the game in Turin, but if the Italians thought they were in pole position they were mistaken; when they were held 0–0 by Belgium in their final group game, it was the Belgians who progressed on goals scored.

A rare spot of bother

West Germany's defeat by Czechoslovakia in the 1976 final remains the only occasion that any German team, at either club or international level, has ever lost a **penalty shoot-out**

In the final Belgium met West Germany, who had gained their revenge over Czechoslovakia and also eliminated Holland in their group thanks to a Klaus Allofs hat-trick. Neutrals in the Rome crowd cheered René Vandereycken's penalty equaliser for Belgium, but the bulky Horst Hrubesch had the last laugh for Germany when he headed home a minute from time.

Platini in Paris: 1984

The finals were hosted by the French and at last given a decent structure that did not discourage adventurous football. France, Portugal, Spain and Denmark qualified for the semi-finals from an eight-team group stage. In Lyon the Danes, who had beaten England at Wembley to qualify, **played some majestic football** but found the Spaniards hard to break down. Spain for their part had already eliminated West Germany with a late António Maceda header despite having not been in the game for long periods. Now they were to do the same again, Maceda cancelling out Søren Lerby's early goal; the Danes eventually lost 4–3 on penalties.

The other semi-final, in Marseille, also looked as though it was going to penalties when France's Jean Tigana went on one final surge to the byline and crossed for skipper Michel Platini to fire home from close range. The final score, 3–2, reflected the see-saw nature of a game often regarded as the best the finals have ever produced. The final did not live up to it, Spanish keeper Luís Arconada letting Platini's lame free-kick go in under his body to set up a 2–0 win for the hosts. But the prize was richly deserved by France and their all-out attacking football.

The future is orange: 1988

After missing out on Euro '84, England returned to the finals in West Germany and were immediately beaten 1–0 by Ireland, making their debut in a big international football tournament. In the end, though, neither side made it through the group stage, Wim Kieft's **lucky late goal** giving Holland victory over the Irish in the last group game when Jack Charlton's team needed only a draw to see them through. The other qualifiers were the Soviet Union, who beat Holland and England to top the group. On the other side of the draw, the host nation and a young but impressive Italy made it into the semi-finals with unbeaten records against Denmark and Spain.

At the first semi in Hamburg, the Germans' tournament came to a sudden end when Marco van Basten's impetuous last-minute strike gave the Dutch a 2–1 win, while a day later in Stuttgart Italy's brave resistance was ended by the USSR. Crucially, Soviet defender Oleg Kuznetsov, who

Content over style

An internet poll in Holland has shown that Dutch fans think their only major honour, the European Championship of 1988, was won with **the worst shirts** *their team has ever worn...*

had brilliantly shackled Dutch playmaker Ruud Gullit in the group-stage meeting between the two countries, was booked during the game and **missed the final** through suspension.

Three days later in Munich, Kuznetsov's absence was brutally exposed by Gullit, who scored one goal and then created the second for van Basten, who had begun the tournament on the bench and ended it by becoming the most celebrated attacking player in the world.

Crashing the party: 1992

The so-called 'friendly finals' were hosted by Sweden, who offered English fans watered-down beer at specially created bars in an attempt to prevent hooliganism. The strategy might have worked, had Graham Taylor not substituted Gary Lineker before the end of his side's last-game defeat (and elimination) by the hosts. Not only was it the end of England's Championship and of England's career, the decision brutally exposed Taylor's own tactical ineptitude.

In the end, both Sweden and their Scandinavian neighbours Denmark qualified for the semi-finals, leaving England and hot favourites France, for whom Michel Platini had turned out to be a surprisingly defence-minded coach, packing their bags early.

In the other group, the **tide of political change** sweeping Europe was evident in two team names: the Commonwealth of Independent States (CIS) travelled to Sweden after having qualified as the Soviet Union, while East and West Germany had united to form plain 'Germany'. Holland and Scotland made up the numbers, and though the Scots played some good football and enjoyed a 3–0 win over the CIS, it wasn't enough to prevent the Dutch and Germans going through.

The biggest political story of all had allowed Denmark into the tournament in preference to Yugoslavia, who had topped their group in qualifying but been suspended because of international sanctions a week before the tournament was due to start. The Danes lacked match-fitness but managed to hold Holland to a 2–2 draw and then win their semi-final on penalties. The other game, equally entertaining, saw Germany edge Sweden 3–2.

Odd man out...

...in this 1992 photo is **Ivica Osim** (third from right) who attended the draw for the finals fully expecting to be in Sweden as coach of Yugoslavia, but whose team were excluded at the last minute, allowing eventual winners Denmark to enter in their place

The hosts may have been out, but in the final Scandinavian rivalry was forgotten as the locals all backed the gatecrashers Denmark against Germany. John Jensen's speculative long-range effort gave the Danes the lead against the run of play on 18 minutes, and Kim Vilfort sealed the most unlikely of wins 12 minutes from the end, to chants of 'Auf Wiedersehen!' from the thousands of Danish fans who had **cancelled their holidays** to back their team in the finals.

The cup goes home – 1996

England hosted the finals for the first time and, with the fall of the Iron Curtain dramatically increasing the number of teams trying to qualify, UEFA bowed to pressure and expanded the competition to 16 teams arranged in four groups of four.

The hosts' progress included an emotional 2–0 win over Scotland and a 4–1 thrashing of Holland, and *Football's Coming Home* swept the nation. Terry Venables' side, with Alan Shearer and Teddy Sheringham a potent strike partnership and Paul Gascoigne in irrepressible form behind them, seemed unstoppable. Inevitably, the Germans had other ideas: Stefan Kuntz cancelled out Shearer's early opener, and though England came desperately close to scoring a 'sudden death' winner in extra time, Germany won the day in a shoot-out.

The Germans' opponents in the final were to be the Czech Republic, who beat Italy, Portugal (with Karel Poborský's wonder-chip) and France (in a shoot-out) on their way to Wembley. The supporters who followed the Czechs to England hadn't banked on staying for longer than the group stage, so financed their extended stay by **betting against their own team's survival**.

In the final, a dubious penalty was converted by Patrik Berger midway through the second half, but this was swiftly cancelled out by an Oliver Bierhoff header for Germany. The advent of sudden-death extra time had been criticised during the tournament because too many teams lacked the guts to come forward. The final would probably have been little different had a freaky deflection not taken Bierhoff's shot past the stranded Petr Kouba to give the Germans a record-breaking third European title.

Highs and Lows – 2000

For the first time in its history, the competition was co-hosted by two nations – Belgium and Holland. Travelling across the Low Countries presented a strange contrast, for whereas the Dutch appeared to be using the tournament as an excuse to hold one **enormous party**, in Belgium you'd have been hard-pushed to tell there was an event on at all. The contrast was reflected in the fate of the two teams, the Belgians failing to progress beyond their group, the Dutch dancing effortlessly into the semi-finals.

England's 1–0 victory over Germany, with Alan Shearer taking what was virtually his team's only goalscoring chance, should have been a cause for celebration among English fans in Charleroi. Instead there were yet more **outbreaks of violence**, driven by a combination of hot weather, strong Belgian ale and sheer pigheadedness.

As it turned out, neither England nor Germany were good enough to reach the knockout stage,

> ### Probably the best...
>
> *Travelling fans at Euro 2000 were delighted to see **beer on sale** at all grounds thanks to Carlsberg's sponsorship of the tournament. But although it was packaged to look like the real thing, the brew was in fact alcohol-free*

their places taken by the more inventive Portugal and Romania. The Portuguese presented the first real test for World Cup holders France, Nuno Gomes putting his team 1–0 up in the Brussels semi-final before Thierry Henry equalised and Abel Xavier's handball on the line, deep into extra time, gifted Zinedine Zidane the chance to put the French into the final from the penalty spot.

The other semi, between Holland and Italy in Amsterdam, somehow failed to produce a goal in two hours of football. The Dutch missed a string of chances including two penalties against a **brazenly unambitious** Italian side, then fluffed two more spot-kicks in the ensuing shoot-out.

In the final, Italy finally showed their more adventurous side and deservedly took the lead through Marco Delvecchio ten minutes into the second half. Alessandro del Piero then missed two clear chances to put his team 2–0 up, before a late, utterly uncharacteristic lapse in the Italian defence allowed Sylvain Wiltord to equalise for France. Devastated by their own lapse of concentration, the Italians then stood statuesque as David Trezeguet nipped in to net the winner 13 minutes into extra time. Another 'golden goal', another trophy for France.

Qualifying results

Of the 16 places up for grabs at the finals, one went automatically to Portugal as hosts. The **remaining 50 teams** were divided into ten groups of five teams each. The teams played each other home and away, with the group winners all qualifying automatically for the finals. The ten second-placed teams went into two-leg play-offs, with the five aggregate winners also qualifying for Euro 2004…

Group 1

FRANCE	8	8	0	0	29-2	24
Slovenia	8	4	2	2	15-12	14
Israel	8	2	3	3	9-11	9
Cyprus	8	2	2	4	9-18	8
Malta	8	0	1	7	5-24	1

7-9-02   Slovenia   3-0   Malta
[Debono 37og, Siljak 59, Cimirotic 90]
          Cyprus   1-2   France
[Okkas 15; Cissé 38, Wiltord 52]

12-10-02 France   5-0   Slovenia
[Vieira 10, Marlet 35, 65, Wiltord 79, Govou 86]
          Malta   0-2   Israel
[Balali 56, Revivo 75]

16-10-02 Israel   ppd   Cyprus
          Malta   0-4   France
[Henry 25, 36, Wiltord 59, Carrière 84]

20-11-02 Cyprus   2-1   Malta
[Rauffmann 49, Okkas 73; Mifsud 90]

29-3-03 Cyprus   1-1   Israel
[Rauffmann 60; Afek 3]
          France   6-0   Malta
[Wiltord 37, Henry 39, 54, Zidane 57pen, 80,
Trezeguet 71]

2-4-03   Slovenia   4-1   Cyprus
[Siljak 4, 14, Zahovic 39pen, N.Ceh 43;
Konstantinou 11]
          Israel   1-2   France
                          [in Palermo]
[Afek 2; Trezeguet 23, Zidane 45]

30-4-03 Malta   1-3   Slovenia
[Mifsud 90; Zahovic 15, Siljak 37, 57]
          Israel   2-0   Cyprus
[Badir 88, Holtsman 90]   [in Palermo]

7-6-03   Israel   0-0   Slovenia
                          [in Antalya]
          Malta   1-2   Cyprus
[Dmiech 72; Konstantinou 23pen, 54]

6-9-03   France   5-0   Cyprus
[Trezeguet 8, 80, Wiltord 21, 41, Henry 60]
          Slovenia   3-1   Israel
[Siljak 35, Knavs 37, N Ceh 78; Revivo 69]

10-9-03 Israel   2-2   Malta
[Revivo 16, Balili 78; Mifsud 51pen,
Carabott 52]   [in Antalya]
          Slovenia   0-2   France
[Trezeguet 9, Dacourt 72]

10-10-03 Cyprus   2-2   Slovenia
[Georgiou 79, Yiasoumi 82; Siljak 12, 42]
          France   3-0   Israel
[Henry 8, Trezeguet 24, Boumsong 42]

Group 2

```
DENMARK . . . . . .8   4   3   1   15-9   15
*Norway . . . . . . .8   4   2   2   9-5   14
Romania . . . . . . .8   4   2   2   21-9   14
Bosnia . . . . . . . .8   4   1   3   7-8   13
Luxembourg . . . .8   0   0   8   0-21   0
```
Norway above Romania on head-to-head record

7-9-02 Norway **2-2** Denmark
[Riise 55, Carew 90+3; Tomasson 23, 71]
Bosnia **0-3** Romania
[Chivu 8, Munteanu 10, Ganea 28]

12-10-02 Denmark **2-0** Luxembourg
[Tomasson 51pen, Sand 71]
Romania **0-1** Norway
[Iversen 84]

16-10-02 Norway **2-0** Bosnia
[Lundekwam 10, Riise 27]
Luxembourg **0-7** Romania
[Moldovan 2, 5, Radoi 24, Contra 45, 47, 86, Ghioane 80]

29-3-03 Bosnia **2-0** Luxembourg
[Bolic 53, Barbarez 75]
Romania **2-5** Denmark
[Mutu 5, Munteanu 47; Rommedahl 9, 90+3, Gravesen 53, Tomasson 71, Contra 73og]

2-4-03 Luxembourg **0-2** Norway
[Rushfeldt 58, Solskjær 73]
Denmark **0-2** Bosnia
[Barbarez 22, Baljic 28]

7-6-03 Denmark **1-0** Norway
[Grønkjær 4]
Romania **2-0** Bosnia
[Mutu 46, Ganea 87]

11-6-03 Luxembourg **0-2** Denmark
[Jensen 22, Gravesen 50]
Norway **1-1** Romania
[Solskjær 78pen; Ganea 64]

6-9-03 Bosnia **1-0** Norway
[Bajramovic 86]
Romania **4-0** Luxembourg
[Mutu 39, Pancu 42, Ganea 43, Bratu 78]

10-9-03 Luxembourg **0-1** Bosnia
[Barbarez 36]
Denmark **2-2** Romania
[Tomasson 34pen, Laursen 90+5; Mutu 62, Pancu 71]

11-10-03 Norway **1-0** Luxembourg
[T A Flo 8]
Bosnia **1-1** Denmark
[Bolic 39; Jørgensen 12]

Group 3

```
CZECH REP . . . . . . . . . .8   7   1   0   23-5   22
Holland . . . . . . . . . . . . . .8   6   1   1   20-6   19
Austria . . . . . . . . . . . . . .8   3   0   5   12-14   9
Moldova . . . . . . . . . . . . .8   2   0   6   5-19   6
Belarus . . . . . . . . . . . . . .8   1   0   7   4-20   3
```

7-9-02 Austria **2-0** Moldova
[Herzog 4pen, 30pen]
Holland **3-0** Belarus
[Davids 35, Kluivert 37, Hasselbaink 74]

12-10-02 Moldova **0-2** Czech Rep
[Jankulovski 70pen, Rosicky 80]
Belarus **0-2** Austria
[Schopp 57, Akagündüz 89]

16-10-02 Austria 0-3 Holland
[Seedorf 16, Cocu 20, Makaay 29]
Czech Rep 2-0 Belarus
[Poborsky 7, Baros 23]

29-3-03 Holland 1-1 Czech Rep
[van Nistelrooy 45; Koller 68]
Belarus 2-1 Moldova
[Kutuzov 42, Gurenko 58; Cebotari 14]

2-4-03 Czech Rep 4-0 Austria
[Nedved 18, Koller 31, 62, Jankulovski 56pen]
Moldova 1-2 Holland
[Boret 16; van Nistelrooy37, van Bommel 84]

7-6-03 Moldova 1-0 Austria
[Frunza 60]
Belarus 0-2 Holland
[Overmars 62, Kluivert 68]

11-6-03 Czech Rep 5-0 Moldova
[Smicer 41, Koller 72pen, Stajner 81, Lokvenc 88, 90+2]
Austria 5-0 Belarus
[Aufhauser 33, Haas 47, Kirchler 52, Wallner 62, Cerny 69]

6-9-03 Holland 3-1 Austria
[van der Vaart 30, Kluivert 60, Cocu 64; Pogatetz 34]
Belarus 1-3 Czech Rep
[Bulyga 13; Nedved 41, Baros 55, Smicer 85]

10-9-03 Czech Rep 3-1 Holland
[Koller 15pen, Poborsky 38, Baros 90+4; van der Vaart 61]
Moldova 2-1 Belarus
[Dadu 26, Covalciuc 89; Vasilyuk 90pen]

11-10-03 Austria 2-3 Czech Rep
[Haas 50, Ovanschitz 78; Jankulovski 26, Vachousek 79, Koller 92]
Holland 5-0 Moldova
[Kluivert 43, Sneijder 51, van Hooijdonk 74pen, van der Vaart 80, Robben 89]

Group 4

SWEDEN	8	5	2	1	19-3	17
Latvia	8	5	1	2	10-6	16
Poland	8	4	1	3	11-7	13
Hungary	8	3	2	3	15-9	11
San Marino	8	0	0	8	0-30	0

7-9-02 San Marino 0-2 Poland
[Kaczorowski 74, Kukielka 88]
Latvia 0-0 Sweden

12-10-02 Sweden 1-1 Hungary
[Ibrahimovic 76; Kenesei 5]
Poland 0-1 Latvia
[Laizans 30]

16-10-02 Hungary 3-0 San Marino
[Gera 49, 61, 89]

20-11-02 San Marino 0-1 Latvia
[Valentini 90og]

29-3-03 Poland 0-0 Hungary

2-4-03 Poland 5-0 San Marino
[Szymkowiak 3, Kosowski 27, Kuzba 54, 90+3, Karwan 82]
Hungary 1-2 Sweden
[Lisztes 65; Allbäck 34, 67]

30-4-03 Latvia 3-0 San Marino
[Prohorenkovs 10, Bleidelis 21, 74]

7-6-03 Hungary 3-1 Latvia
[Szabics 51, 59, Gera 86; Verpakovskis 38]
San Marino 0-6 Sweden
[Jonson 16, 59, 70, Allbäck 54, 85, Ljungberg 68]

11-6-03 Sweden 3-0 Poland
[Svensson 16, 71, Allbäck 43]
San Marino 0-5 Hungary
[Böör 5, Lisztes 20, 82, Kenesei 62, Szabics 77]

6-9-03   Latvia   0-2   Poland
[Szymkowiak 36, Klos 39]
    Sweden   5-0   San Marino
[Jonsson 32, Jakobsson 48, Ibrahimovic 56, 83pen, Källström 68pen]

10-9-03   Poland   0-2   Sweden
[Nilsson 2, Mellberg 37]
    Latvia   3-1   Hungary
[Verpakovskis 38, 51, Astafjevs 43; Lisztes 52]

11-10-03   Sweden   0-1   Latvia
[Verpakovskis 23]
    Hungary   1-2   Poland
[Szabics 46; Niedzielan 10, 62]

Group 5

GERMANY	8	5	3	0	13-4	18
Scotland	8	4	2	2	12-8	14
Iceland	8	4	1	3	11-9	13
Lithuania	8	3	1	4	7-11	10
Faroe Isles	8	0	1	7	7-18	1

Torsten Frings and Colin Cameron get physical, Glasgow, June 03

7-9-02   Faroe Isles   2-2   Scotland
[Petersen 6, 11; Lambert 62, Ferguson 84]
    Lithuania   0-2   Germany
[Ballack 27, Stankevicius 59og]

12-10-02   Iceland   0-2   Scotland
[Dailly 7, Naysmith 62]
    Lithuania   2-0   Faroe Isles
[Razanauskas 23pen, Poskus 37]

16-10-02   Germany   2-1   Faroe Isles
[Ballack 2pen, Klose 59; Friedrich 45og]
    Iceland   3-0   Lithuania
[Helgason 50, Gudjohnsen 60, 73]

29-3-03   Scotland   2-1   Iceland
[Miller 12, Wilkie 70; Gudjohnsen 49]
    Germany   1-1   Lithuania
[Ramelow 9; Razanauskas 73]

2-4-03   Lithuania   1-0   Scotland
[Razanauskas 74pen]

7-6-03   Scotland   1-1   Germany
[Miller 69; Bobic 22]
    Iceland   2-1   Faroe Isles
[Sigurdsson 50, Gudmundsson 90+2; Jacobsen 61]

11-6-03   Faroe Isles   0-2   Germany
[Klose 89, Bobic 90+2]
    Lithuania   0-3   Iceland
[Gudjonsson 60, Gudjohnsen 72, Hreidarsson 90+4]

20-8-03   Faroe Isles   1-2   Iceland
[Jacobsen 67; Gudjohnsen 6, Marteinsson 71]

6- 9-03   Scotland   3-1   Faroe Isles
[McCann 8, Dickov 45+2, McFadden 74; Johnsson 35]

          Iceland   0-0   Germany

10-9-03   Faroe Isles   1-3   Lithuania
[Olsen 43; Morinas 21, 58, Vencevicius 88]

          Germany   2-1   Scotland
[Bobic 26, Ballack 50pen; McCann 60]

11-10-03 Scotland   1-0   Lithuania
[Fletcher 70]

          Germany   3-0   Iceland
[Ballack 9, Bobic 59, Kuranyi 79]

Group 6

GREECE	8	6	0	2	8-4	18
Spain	8	5	2	1	16-4	17
Ukraine	8	2	4	2	11-10	10
Armenia	8	2	1	6	7-16	7
N Ireland	8	0	3	5	0-8	3

7-9-02   Greece   0-2   Spain
[Raúl 8, Valerón 76]

          Armenia   2-2   Ukraine
[Petrosian 75, Sarkisian 87; Serebrennikov 2, Zubov 33]

12-10-02 Spain   3-0   N Ireland
[Baraja 19, 88, Guti 59]

          Ukraine   2-0   Greece
[Vorobei 50, Voronin 90]

16-10-02 Greece   2-0   Armenia
[Nikolaidis 2, 60]

          N Ireland   0-0   Ukraine

29-3-03   Armenia   1-0   N Ireland
[Petrosian 86]

          Ukraine   2-2   Spain
[Voronin 12, Horshkov 90; Raúl 83, Etxebarría 86]

2-4-03   N Ireland   0-2   Greece
[Charisteas 4, 56]

          Spain   3-0   Armenia
[Tristán 65, Helguera 70, Joaquín 90]

7-6-03   Spain   0-1   Greece
[Giannakopoulos 43]

          Ukraine   4-3   Armenia
[Horshkov 28, Shevchenko 66pen, 73, Fedorov 90+2; Sarkisian 14pen, Petrosian 74]

11-6-03   N Ireland   0-0   Spain

          Greece   1-0   Ukraine
[Charisteas 86]

6-9-03   Armenia   0-1   Greece
[Vryzas 36]

          Ukraine   0-0   N Ireland

10-9-03   N Ireland   0-1   Armenia
[Arm Karamian 27]

          Spain   2-1   Ukraine
[Raúl 60, 70; Shevchenko 84]

11-10-03 Greece   1-0   N Ireland
[Tsartas 77]

          Armenia   0-4   Spain
[Valerón 7, Raúl 78, Reyes 86, 90]

Group 7

ENGLAND	8	6	2	0	14-5	20
Turkey	8	6	1	1	17-5	19
Slovakia	8	3	1	4	11-9	10
Macedonia	8	1	3	4	11-14	6
Liechtenstein	8	0	1	7	2-22	1

7-9-02   Turkey   3-0   Slovakia
[Serhat 14, Arif 45, 65]

8-9-02   Liechtenstein 1-1   Macedonia
[Mi Stocklasa 90; Hristov 8]

12-10-02 Slovakia   1-2   England
[Nemeth 23; Beckham 65, Owen 82]
     Macedonia   1-2   Turkey
[Grozdanovski 2; Okan 29, Nihat 54]

16-10-02 Turkey   5-0   Liechtenstein
[Okan 7, Ümit 17, Ilhan 22, Serhat 82, 90]
     England   2-2   Macedonia
[Beckham 14, Gerrard 36; Sakiri 11, Trajanov 25]

29-3-03 Liechtenstein 0-2   England
[Owen 28, Beckham 53]
     Macedonia   0-2   Slovakia
[Petras 28, Reiter 90]

2-4-03 England   2-0   Turkey
[Vassell 75, Beckham 90pen]
     Slovakia   4-0   Liechtenstein
[Reiter 18, Nemeth 51, 65, Janocko 90]

7-6-03 Slovakia   0-1   Turkey
[Nihat 12]
     Macedonia   3-1   Liechtenstein
[Sedloski 39pen, Krstev 51, Stojkov 80; Beck 19]

11-6-03 England   2-1   Slovakia
[Owen 62pen, 73; Janocko 31]
     Turkey   3-2   Macedonia
[Nihat 27, Gökdeniz 48, Hakan 59; Grozdanovski 23, Sakiri 29]

6-9-03 Liechtenstein 0-3   Turkey
[Tümer 14, Okan 41, Hakan 50]
     Macedonia   1-2   England
[Hristov 28; Rooney 53, Beckham 63pen]

10-9-03 England   2-0   Liechtenstein
[Owen 46, Rooney 52]
     Slovakia   1-1   Macedonia
[Nemeth 25; Dimitrovski 62]

11-10-03 Turkey   0-0   England
     Liechtenstein 0-2   Slovakia
[Vittek 40, 56]

Group 8

BULGARIA	8	5	2	1	13-4	17
*Croatia	8	5	1	2	12-4	16
Belgium	8	5	1	2	11-9	16
Estonia	8	2	2	4	4-6	8
Andorra	8	0	0	8	1-18	0

Croatia ahead of Belgium on head-to-head record

7-9-02 Belgium   0-2   Bulgaria
[Jankovic 17, S Petrov 65]
     Croatia   0-0   Estonia

12-10-02 Andorra   0-1   Belgium
[Sonck 62]
     Bulgaria   2-0   Croatia
[Petrov 21, Berbatov 37]

16-10-02 Estonia   0-1   Belgium
[Sonck 2]
     Bulgaria   2-1   Andorra
[Chilikov 33, Balakov 58; A Lima 80]

29-3-03 Croatia   4-0   Belgium
[Srna 9, Prso 53, T Maric 68, Leko 76]

Belgium's defenders argue about how best to arrange their wall, August 03

2-4-03   Estonia   0-0   Bulgaria
            Croatia   2-0   Andorra
[Rapaic 11pen, 44]

30-4-03   Andorra   0-2   Estonia
[Zelinski 28, 75]

7-6-03   Bulgaria   2-2   Belgium
[Berbatov 52, Todorov 71pen; St Petrov 31og, Clement 56]
            Estonia   2-0   Andorra
[Allas 22, Viikmäe 31]

11-6-03   Estonia   0-1   Croatia
[N Kovac 77]
            Belgium   3-0   Andorra
[Goor 20, 68, Sonck 44]

6-9-03   Bulgaria   2-0   Estonia
[M Petrov 16, Berbatov 68]
            Andorra   0-3   Croatia
[N Kovac 6, Simunic 17, Rosso 71]

10-9-03   Belgium   2-1   Croatia
[Sonck 35, 43; Simic 36]
            Andorra   0-3   Bulgaria
[Berbatov 11, 24, Hristov 58]

11-10-03   Croatia   1-0   Bulgaria
[Olic 48]
            Belgium   2-0   Estonia
[Reinumäe 44og, Buffel 60]

Group 9

ITALY	8	5	2	1	17-4	17
Wales	8	4	1	3	13-10	13
*Serbia/M'negro.	8	3	3	2	11-11	12
Finland	8	3	1	4	9-10	10
Azerbaijan	8	1	1	6	5-20	4

Serbia/Montenegro competed as Yugoslavia until February 2003

7-9-02   Azerbaijan   0-2   Italy
[Achemedov 33og, Del Piero 64]
            Finland   0-2   Wales
[Hartson 31, Davies 73]

12-10-02   Finland   3-0   Azerbaijan
[Nurmela 13, Tihinen 59, Hyypiä 71]
            Italy   1-1   Yugoslavia
[Del Piero 39; Mijatovic 27]

16-10-02   Wales   2-1   Italy
[Davies 12, Bellamy 73; del Piero 32]
            Yugoslavia   2-0   Finland
[Kovacevic 54, Mihajlovic 84]

20-11-02   Azerbaijan   0-2   Wales
[Speed 9, Hartson 68]

12-2-03   Serbia/M'gro   2-2   Azerbaijan
[Mijatovic 34pen, Lazetic 52; Gurbanov 59, 78]

29-3-03   Italy   2-0   Finland
[Vieri 6, 24]
            Wales   4-0   Azerbaijan
[Akhmedov 1og, Speed 40, Hartson 44, Giggs 52]

7-6-03   Finland   3-0   Serbia/M'gro
[Hyypiä 19, Kolkka 45, Forssell 56]

11-6-03   Finland   0-2   Italy
[Totti 32, Del Piero 73]
            Azerbaijan   2-1   Serbia/M'gro
[Gurbanov 88pen, Izmailov 90+1; Boskovic 27]

20-8-03   Serbia/M'gro   1-0   Wales
[Mladenovic 73]

6-9-03   Azerbaijan   1-2   Finland
[Izmailov 88; Tainio 52, Nurmela 74]
            Italy   4-0   Wales
[Inzaghi 59, 63, 70, Del Piero 76pen]

10-9-03   Wales   1-1   Finland
[Davies 3; Forssell 80]
            Serbia/M'gro   1-1   Italy
[Ilic 82; Inzaghi 22]

11-10-03 Italy   4-0   Azerbaijan
[Vieri 16, F Inzaghi 24, 88, di Vaio 65]
Wales   2-3   Serbia/M'gro
[Hartson 26pen, Earnshaw 90+2; Vukic 4,
Milosevic 82, Ljuboja 87]

Group 10

```
SWITZERLAND .. 8   4   3   1   15-11   15
Russia ........ 8   4   2   2   19-12   14
Ireland ........ 8   3   2   3   10-11   11
Albania........ 8   2   2   4   11-15    8
Georgia........ 8   2   1   5    8-14    7
```

7-9-02   Russia   4-2   Ireland
[Kariaka 20, Beschastnykh 25, Kerzhakov 69,
Babb 86og; Docherty 68, Morrison 75]

8- 9-02   Switzerland   4-1   Georgia
[Frey 37, H Yakin 63, Müller 74, Chapuisat 82;
S Arveladze 62]

12-10-02 Albania   1-1   Switzerland
[Murati 79; H Yakin 37]
          Georgia   abd   Russia

16-10-02 Ireland   1-2   Switzerland
[Magnin 77og; Yakin 45, Celestini 87]
          Russia   4-1   Albania
[Kerzhakov 3, Semak 41, 54, Onopko 52; Duro 15]

29-3-03   Albania   3-1   Russia
[Rraklli 21, Lala 79, Tare 82; Kariaka 77]
          Georgia   1-2   Ireland
[Kobiashvili 60; Duff 18, Doherty 85]

2-4-03   Albania   0-0   Ireland
          Georgia   0-0   Switzerland

30-4-03   Georgia   1-0   Russia
[Asatiana 11]

Shota Arveladze and Colin Healy
invent a new dance move, June 03

7-6-03   Ireland   2-1   Albania
[Robbie Keane 6, Aliaj 90+2og; Skela 8]
Switzerland   2-2   Russia
[Frei 14, 16; Ignashevich 24, 68pen]

11-6-03   Ireland   2-0   Georgia
[Doherty 43, Robbie Keane 59]
Switzerland   3-2   Albania
[Haas 10, Frei 32, Cabanas 72; Lala 23,
Skela 86pen]

6-9-03   Georgia   3-0   Albania
[S Arveladze 9, 44, Ashvetia 18]
          Ireland   1-1   Russia
[Duff 35; Ignashevich 42]

10-9-03   Albania   3-1   Georgia
[Hasi 50, Tare 52, Bushi 79; S Arveladze 62]
          Russia   4-1   Switzerland
[Bulykin 20, 32, 59, Mostovoi 72; Karyaka 13og]

11-10-03 Russia   3-1   Georgia
[Bulykin 30, Titov 45, Sychev 72; Iashvili 3]
          Switzerland   2-0   Ireland
[H Yakin 6, Frei 60]

Turkish players blame each other for allowing Latvia to get a goal back in Istanbul, November 03

Play-offs

First legs: 15-11-03

Latvia	1-0	Turkey

[Verpakovskis 29]

Scotland	1-0	Holland

[McFadden 22]

Croatia	1-1	Slovenia

[Prso 5; Siljak 22]

Russia	0-0	Wales
Spain	2-1	Norway

[Raúl 21, Baraja 85; Iversen 14]

Second legs: 19-11-03

Turkey	2-2	Latvia

[Ilhan 20, Hakan 64; Laizans 66, Verpakovskis 78]

Holland	6-0	Scotland

[Sneijder 14, Ooijer 32,
van Nistelrooy 37, 51, 67, F de Boer 65]

Slovenia	0-1	Croatia

[Prso 61]

Wales	0-1	Russia

[Evseev 22]

Norway	0-3	Spain

[Raúl 34, Vicente 49, Etxebarría 56]

LATVIA, HOLLAND, CROATIA, RUSSIA and SPAIN qualify for finals

Match schedule

At the finals, the 16 competing teams are divided into four groups of four, who play each other once. The **top two teams** in each group proceed to the knockout stage. All kick-off times given below are local time, which is the same as UK time.

Group A

12-6-04	Portugal	v	Greece	Porto (Dragão), 17:00
	Spain	v	Russia	Faro, 19:45
16-6-04	Greece	v	Spain	Porto (Bessa), 17:00
	Russia	v	Portugal	Lisbon (Luz), 19:45
20-6-04	Spain	v	Portugal	Lisbon (José Alvalade), 19:45
	Russia	v	Greece	Faro, 19:45

Group B

13-6-04	Switzerland	v	Croatia	Leiria, 17:00
	France	v	England	Lisbon (Luz), 19:45
17-6-04	England	v	Switzerland	Coimbra, 17:00
	Croatia	v	France	Leiria, 19:45
21-6-04	Croatia	v	England	Lisbon (Luz), 19:45
	Switzerland	v	France	Coimbra, 19:45

Group C

14-6-04	Denmark	v	Italy	Guimarães, 17:00
	Sweden	v	Bulgaria	Lisbon (José Alvalade), 19:45
18-6-04	Bulgaria	v	Denmark	Braga, 17:00
	Italy	v	Sweden	Porto (Dragão), 19:45
22-6-04	Italy	v	Bulgaria	Guimarães, 19:45
	Denmark	v	Sweden	Porto (Bessa), 19:45

Group D

15-6-04	Czech Rep	v	Latvia	Aveiro, 17:00
	Germany	v	Netherlands	Porto (Dragão), 19:45
19-6-04	Germany	v	Latvia	Porto (Bessa), 17:00
	Netherlands	v	Czech Rep	Aveiro, 19:45
23-6-04	Netherlands	v	Latvia	Braga, 19:45
	Germany	v	Czech Rep	Lisbon (José Alvalade), 19:45

Match schedule (continued)

Quarter-finals

24-6-04	Winners A	v	Runners-up B	Lisbon (Luz), 19:45
25-6-04	Winners B	v	Runners-up A	Lisbon (José Alvalade), 19:45
26-6-04	Winners C	v	Runners-up D	Faro, 19:45
27-6-04	Winners D	v	Runners-up C	Porto (Dragão), 19:45

Semi-finals

30-6-04	Winners 24 June	v	Winners 26 June	Lisbon (José Alvalade), 19:45
1-7-04	Winners 25 June	v	Winners 27 June	Porto (Dragão), 19:45

Final

4-7-04	Winners 30 June	v	Winners July 1	Lisbon (Luz), 19:45